Trout and Trouting

Trout and Trouting

David Scholes
Photographs by Peter Whyte

Kangaroo Press

The author in action, 1993

To Dear Patricia

Also by David Scholes:

Fly Fisher in Tasmania
The Way of an Angler
Trout Quest
Tasmanian Angler
Fly Fishing in Australia
Trutta the Trout
Trout Days
Ripples, Runs and Rises
Fly Fishing Pictorial (with Tony Ritchie)

First published in 1993 by Kangaroo Press Pty Ltd
3 Whitehall Road (P.O. Box 75) Kenthurst NSW 2156 Australia
Typeset by G.T. Setters Pty Limited
Printed in Singapore by Kyodo Printing Co (S'pore) Pte Ltd

ISBN 0 86417 540 X

Contents

Preface

Not long ago a dying angler telephoned me from his hospital bed in Melbourne to tell me how much he had enjoyed reading my book *The Way of an Angler*, and how for short periods it had transported him, as it were, to the streamside where he shared my triumphs and defeats and my contentment. Indeed, he told me, he was able to forget his unhappy situation altogether during these all too brief respites and felt that he was there with me wading the stream, feeling the warm sun on his back, seeing the quiet rise beside the strapweed under the far bank and making a long cast to drop his Red Tag in a space between the strands.

I do not know his name. All I know is that his throat had been so invaded by cancer that most of it had been removed, he was fed liquids by tube and his voice was best described as a raspy slur. At first I thought it was some sort of a hoax call, or a drunk who had dialed my number in error. But, no, here he was lying there in his bed, the telephone held in place by a nurse; while using some sort of artificial voice-box he spoke to me as best he could: 'David,' he said, 'you've done me good. You've restored my soul and I just wanted to say hello and thank you.'

Well, what would you have said? What did I say? I know that I thanked him but what else I said escapes my memory. I know that my mind was racing and that I was at once filled with a profound pity. But also I recall a warmth or gratification that I had been able to give him comfort. But what really moved me—yes, touched my heart, if you like—was his poor, shaky, weak voice telling me that I had restored his soul! I only know of one other such phrase and I refer you to the Twenty-third Psalm. What a warmth I have felt since that time whenever I think about it. That this unfortunate man, knowing that he was not going to live long, never again to see the sparkle of a trout stream or hear its rippling music, crunch over its pebbly margins or drink from its cold, clear shallows, was refreshed by what I had written is more than just recompense; it is a great solace.

So there it is. Largely as a result of this experience, together with others when I have received both pleasant reports and a spurring on to more of the same, I am persuaded to try one more time to write further trouty words with the hope that they might again bring smiles to some and peace of mind to others. My thoughts as I write have ranged widely, so I have grouped those of similar theme under several headings to form chapters and more organised and engaging reading.

Come, then, let's fish together.

David Scholes
Launceston
Tasmania

1 Sounds and Sidelights

You know those pretty little yellow daisies called happiness that flower in the late spring when in places they become a spectacular golden carpet across the fields, and are so soft that even when you get yourself hooked up in one it's easy to get yourself unhooked? Well, after Christmas when they die and dry out they become thoroughly horrible things with thin wiry stalks, while the flower shrivels up into a grey-brown head, the whole article acquiring the strength of steel. Never will they let go. Never. You must go down to it and break it. And even then it may grasp the fly so tenaciously that you must use both hands. Almost certainly you will be angry, which is not a good way to return to your casting.

Now that I'm talking about hangups I had better keep at it. Surely nobody gets hooked up as much as I do. Both behind and in front. Even at a rod's length I can do it with both consistency and ease. Scotch thistles are bad. And blackberries. And gorse. And those awful things that grow out of strapweed, covered with bulbous green pods all round. And hawthorn. And briars. But all of them are twice as bad when dry. Pretty they might be, but they try me sorely. Willows, gums and often wattles are not as bad; with luck you can frequently pull free.

But many a time there you are with a broken point and a lost fly. Out comes the repair gear and with a not-too-happy disposition down you plonk to tie a bloodknot. Do you get all hot and bothered on hot days? Your fingers are nowhere near as nimble as when you first tied the fly on. There was a time when I fished the evening rise until dark and sometimes had to tie a knot at night. For this I carried a little torch and knelt on my knees to do the job. But compared to the sweat and swoon and irk of tying the same knot on a hot day, it was easy. And what about those little black flies that walk up and down your nose on hot days and investigate the very corners of your eyes just as you try to poke the end through? My stars, it's a ticklish business.

'Pretty little yellow daisies'

Are you a good knot tyer? I know a chap who can tie perfect bloodknots in a flash. But he cuts the ends off too short. Well, too short for me that is. I always leave a millimetre or so, the trout don't mind. But when you're hooked up on some thorny bramble and you give the fly a bit of a yank to free it and bang goes the leader at a knot because it's come undone, you're none too delighted I'll wager.

On windy days—which I know all about—I sometimes get hooked up in myself. Mostly it happens when I'm trying to grasp the fly to hook it in the ring. Suddenly a fiendish gust comes and, before I know it, the fly darts over my shoulder to fix itself to the back of my shirt or jumper. If you're by yourself and if, like me, you're not a contortionist the resultant struggle to get the hook free is as good as an afternoon at the circus. But I get flies stuck in my front half too. In my trousers, even in my socks. I'm good at it.

I once knew a doctor—alas no longer with us—who, while fishing in New Zealand, caught a cow on his backcast. He didn't get his fly back, because the cow just kept on walking. However he tried. I have never hooked a cow. I've been stuck in numerous bridges, boats and buildings—even my car. But every now and then something inexplicable occurs. Even in hookups. The other day I was fast in a small hawthorn. Due to the breeze, which got me up the tree in the first place, every time I succeeded in getting one end clear, as soon as I began on the other it would blow back again. At length I ruefully just put the rod down and called for aid from my nearby wife. On arrival she picked up the rod to assess the position. Lifting the whole lot clear she said with a detectable hint of coldness, 'What's wrong, it's not caught anywhere!'

Wonders never cease.

We all like to watch a hawk in flight or some other bird of prey. How often have you been out in the country with a friend—angler or not—and you come across a hawk swooping low or wheeling high and are at once aware of its superb flight; there are few things more fair! Or perhaps as you pass in your car you can spot a hawk sitting majestically on a post or busy feeding at the roadside on some animal unlucky enough to meet such an unnatural death. Do you know that some people drive purposely over them? They do. Anything that moves. Even in daylight. I do not care for these people. But for the creatures not killed instantly and left to die, perhaps slowly, I care a lot. Some of these dead things are hawks. Not many, however, they are too agile.

There are some seventeen hawks known to occur in Tasmania. Of these about the most common are the brown hawk *Falco berigora* and the swamp hawk *Cirus approximans*. Both are found in open sheep country, along river flats and marshes.

Both have a habit of perching on telegraph poles and dead trees along roads from which they look down disdainfully, seldom bothering to fly. The brown hawk is slightly larger than the swamp hawk and, although it is migratory, Tasmania can rightly claim to have it in greater abundance than other parts of Australia.

Fourteen species of bird are accepted as being endemic to Tasmania but none of these is a hawk. It is clear that the existence of Bass Strait has exerted a considerable influence on the number and variety of birds occurring in Tasmania, seemingly accounting for the absence of several kinds well known in nearby mainland states, and also some that are scattered very widely over the farthest parts of the continent. Among those that have not crossed the strait and become established in Tasmania is the yellow robin. As a boy I fished the Upper Yarra a great deal and got to know and admire them because of their numbers. They were always in pairs. I can see them now. Oh, what days I had.

Talking of birds reminds me about one of the bravest actions in nature that I have ever seen. I was returning from fishing towards Cressy when I came upon a mother plover and three small chicks right in the middle of the road. Without hesitation that plover turned directly towards my oncoming vehicle, and spreading her wings out sideways, feet firmly planted astride, head lowered and eyes blazing, she shrieked loudly for me to halt or else. Which I did. Whereupon she gathered her bewildered little children together and led them to safety. What defiant heroism! What motherly love! Yet, there are some people today who would have run her down. Their souls must be very dull.

And, still on birds, we have in our orchard area some ten pear trees. Every year in March, just when the fruit is ripe enough for them to enjoy, we are invaded by a flock of big currawongs, or jays. And they stay until the last pear and the last bit of anything else to eat is finished before departing. But you can be quite sure that they will be back when the pears are ready. Where do they go and how do they know exactly when to return and where our trees are? Wonderful.

But there is no such admiration for the occasional feral cat that visits us from the nearby bush. Here and there one finds a pitiful little heap of feathers—all that remains of some delightful bird that has fallen foul of one of these sly slinking marauders. Using the leavings from a barbecued chicken as bait I sometimes trap and shoot one, but they are often too cunning to be tempted. Indeed, cats of any kind that kill our birdlife are liable to get shot. I know that nature is red in tooth and claw and it is natural for the feline family to hunt and kill. But let me assure you I'm on the side of the little wrens and honeyeaters, the lovely parrots and raucous wattlebirds. Cats are not my friends.

Birds are beautifully designed and the colouring of their plumage is superb. As with flowers, it's never out of harmony in tint, tone or amount. And the shapes. And the differences, sometimes subtle, between male and female. As an artist I find it all most splendid and bow in acclamation to the great designer.

Some time after World War II the whole fly-fishing for trout scene began to change. And now, today, nearly fifty years on, I am writing to many readers— possibly most—who do not understand some of my thoughts and accounts of what was and what, in my view, should now be. But then I am perplexed that, while I have seen what I have seen, been where I have been and basked at times in the most superb fishing imaginable, I am uncertain whether the modern fly-fisher, who has grown up quite unfamiliar with what I have experienced, would want to duplicate my adventures or enjoy them.

While I find no problem understanding and really living the tales of fortune and disaster told by John Hills in *A Summer on the Test*, Plunket Greene in *Where the Bright Waters Meet*, Vincent Marinaro in *A Modern Dry-fly Code* or a host of others concerning their days on the stream sixty or more years ago, I just wonder how I relate to today's young fly-fishers. Their style of fishing and tackle are sometimes so at variance with those of yesterday that they will need their imagination when I get going. What I am saying is that, while I can feel at home with fly-fishing right back to its beginnings, I rather think that today's angler cannot, indeed he is not much interested anyway. I may be wrong, but consider for a moment the float tube chap, the weighted lure dragging along the bottom method or the downstream skater. If this is the way someone is brought up, then where am I with my balmy spring morning on a flat mayfly stream? Yet, in spite of such apprehension, I know that all ears are not deaf.

I am fortunate in still having a few fishing friends who put skill before kill. But these days it's all numbers. When an angler returns home and opens the door the first thing he's asked is 'How many did you get?' Then it's 'How big were they?' Then 'How big was the biggest?' Then, if you were out with Bill, 'How many did Bill get?' Then 'Were you amongst them all day?' The size of the bag is the measure of the outing. And it's some kind of disgrace to come home troutless. And if Bill caught the most, then he's the best fisherman. How different when I returned to the keeper's cottage in Scotland. 'Did you have a good day?' By which they meant did I have a happy day. Or more recently to that old sage Max Christensen's home. 'Did you get a fish?' was Max's query. A fish note, not how many. If ever asked how many he'd caught his standard one-word reply was 'Enough'.

Over the past decade or so, in keeping with the great increase in popularity

'Balmy spring morning'

of all forms of outdoor activity, trout fishing has received much attention and claimed the interest of many people, fly-fishing included. Here, I suspect, is where the rot set in because instead of coming to it progressively perhaps from boyhood trying various methods, first with bait on the bottom, spinning, trolling, wet fly and then dry fly, many aspirants thought fly-fishing was for them and hey presto! No wonder we have so many instant experts; we live in an instant world where everything worthwhile has got to be *now*. No need to bother with yesterday. First thing is to catch a trout, then a lot of trout, then a big trout—a trophy trout. And so to keep pace and supply the demand fisheries authorities, and in countries like Britain private enterprise also, have stocked waters with large hatchery-reared rainbow trout, while some places can still offer big wild fish. And so on.

I want now to show you both sides of the coin. Fishing magazines have had a heyday during this time. Where before there were but one or two, now there are many. And, as might be expected, the glossy covers show today's style of angler displaying a large trout purposely held towards the camera to look even larger. And all about how he caught it is told inside, plus more pictures, in colour of course. So distasteful do I find this trout pornography that if a copy is passed on to me, I rarely open it. Yesterday, however, I did and glanced over an article on Tasmanian trout by an Australian writer who is at the big fish stage in his angling life, or possibly at the big numbers and big fish stage simultaneously, and tells the reader that big trout are what it's all about, that the ultimate is to catch yourself a whale of a trout and I imagine have it mounted and displayed on the wall for all to see and admire.

I think I know how he feels because I recall some thirty or forty years ago having my own eye on big trout when I enjoyed a heavy bag on my shoulder. But fortunately this outlook was very quickly erased by meeting and fishing with such a fine band of true anglers as Wigram, Christensen, Gibson, Clayton and others.

The other side of the coin is wonderfully pictured by the late Robert Traver, writing in an American fly-fishing magazine, telling me why he goes fishing. If you're like me, after reading it, a kind of gentle refreshment flows over you and the loveliness of fly-fishing shines through the words and your thoughts as you drift into the world of memories and reminiscence. This is my side of the coin to which I will cling forever.

> I fish because I love to; because I love the environs where trout are found, which are invariably beautiful, and hate the environs where crowds of people are found, which are invariably ugly; because of all the television commercials, cocktail parties, and assorted social posturing I thus escape; because in a world where most men

seem to spend their lives doing things they hate, my fishing is at once an endless source of delight and an act of small rebellion; because trout do not lie or cheat and cannot be bought or bribed or impressed by power but respond only to quietude and humility and endless patience; because I suspect that men are going along this way for the last time, and I for one don't want to waste the trip; because mercifully there are no telephones on trout waters; because only in the woods can I find solitude without loneliness; because bourbon out of an old tin cup always tastes better out there; because maybe one day I will catch a mermaid; and, finally, not because I regard fishing as being terribly important but because I suspect that so many of the other concerns of men are equally unimportant—and not nearly so much fun.

I once had a visit from two Victorian fly-fishers who wanted to know where they could go to enjoy fishing in a mountain stream away from people, where they could use dry flies only and catch free-rising panfish. I could have sent them to any one of five or six places, but chose a secluded corner of the upper South Esk, where they could park their caravan almost at the water's edge.

At the end of the week they returned filled with gratitude which filled me with a warmth that, by chance, I had picked just the right place. And they told me it wasn't the beauty of the stream that they found so pleasant, nor the plentiful trout that rose almost in front of their camp, which they had fresh-fried in butter for breakfast, nor the wild foxgloves that grew just beside their caravan, nor the great variety of birdlife, nor the possums that came inside at night to beg titbits from their dinner table, nor the clean, fresh morning air, the blue sky and open fields, nor the gathering purple evening shadows, nor the delicious mushrooms and white wine, nor the clarity of the water as it glided over stones of ochre, burnt sienna and amber, nor the peace and tranquility as they bathed quite naked. No, it was the gurgle of the stream as they lay in their beds for sleep, the chatter and sound of water on rocks that gently lulled them into the realm of dreamland.

In an earlier book I said something about anticipation being half as good as the real thing. Well it is. Thus it is that the first day of the fishing season is one of the happiest dates in the angler's year, for after several cold, dark winter months he's off again filled with hope and enthusiasm. Cold it may be and the wind may still have a bit of its penetrating winter bite, but all around us the country is stirring into life. The cuckoo has been with us for a fortnight past, some deciduous trees are in bud, others in blossom. It's hard to remember the shortest day of the year and its associated melancholy. The whole season lies ahead, and it's a good feeling.

But I'm not only talking about anticipation of the new season. No, this feeling of good things to come lends a special charm to fishing. Old Fred Stewart, well into his sixties, used to say to me that he was just as excited each time we set out as he was as a boy in Scotland. Read what C.F. Walker has to say about it in *Brown Trout and Dry Fly*.

> Sometimes I think anticipation plays a greater part in our enjoyment of fishing than most of us realize: indeed I am not at all sure that it is not the best part of all, for it never lets us down. In anticipation, flies always hatch, trout always rise, and we never make any of those idiotic mistakes from which, alas, few of us are free when it comes to actual fishing.

Now here's a funny thing—have a think about it yourself—most of your really good days are unexpected. You can anticipate all you like but it's never quite like that. Almost every time something goes wrong with what you had in mind. Mostly it's the wind that messes things up, by either being there at all or blowing in the wrong direction. Sometimes it's dull when you want sun, the fly is too thin or the water is at the wrong height. But most good days, I seem to recall, are the result of a wind that drops out or a hatch that comes on. Unexpectedly, that is.

Anticipation does not seem to apply to tackle. You can't imagine how a new rod will work until you've tried it. Nor a fly you've tied. Nor a new kind of line or fly floatant. No, I'm thinking about the anticipation associated with revisiting a stretch of water fished previously, perhaps often, when you know every turn and pool, and in your mind's eye you can see it and you plan how to fish the spot this time, not making the same mistakes again, and you visualise that good one you missed, or pricked, or rolled, under that overhanging wattle. How this time you'll cross over below him and try from that side with a flat sidecast that should overcome the problem of drag; if you miss him on the strike how disgusted you'll be with yourself. And then there's that long straight stretch, with the stony bottom, the left bank the deepest and best, with little bays of protruding ferns where each cast is expectant as the fly rides cheekily down the ripple. And there, at the head of run, where the flow comes in on the other bank, is that slack water on this side, where right at the very extremity, in the shallows, demanding the most accurate of casts, your fly is taken almost as soon as it lands, by a plump pounder that first splashes and then tears off down the run while, as if in applause, a pair of kookaburras laugh loudly from a nearby shady gum. Are you not there? Do you not hear them?

'Long straight stretch with a stony bottom'

2 Life and Lifelike

If the thin ice on which I'm now skating breaks, I'll land in hot water not cold. Many times I have brought entomology into my writings, emphasising its importance in fishing and talking at some length about the natural and its best imitation. To be fair, however, I have also had a good deal to say about it not being so important what you fish as the way you fish it. At any rate the other day I tipped out all the over two hundred dry flies I always carry onto the sunroom table and just sat and looked at them. Supposing, I thought, I pick out those I consider essential to make up a small single box.

First I'll tell you what I chose and then have a word or two about each. Without hesitation I picked up a Red Tag and then one of Noel Jetson's Black Spinners. In what order the rest came I'm not sure, but in went Barry Lodge's Q-dun and Max Christensen's Macquarie Red, a small Dark Alder and a deer-hair Grasshopper. A Senator's Choice, an Iron Blue Dun and a small Black Ant, a Hare's Ear and Gold plus a floating nymph. Lastly I included Dick Woodard's Dragonfly and no more. That made twelve patterns and I carry hundreds! Now let's look at my little collection more closely.

What a magnificent nondescript we have in the Red Tag. I use it in sizes 12 and 14 for general fishing, finding it highly successful just about anytime anywhere and fish it more than any other pattern. For big rough water, or when grasshoppers are about, I have sometimes used a size 10. And most of us know how testing, even exasperating, hatches of caenids can be. They are quite common each late spring or early summer on both streams and lakes. A great number of semi-successful flies have been devised and many words written about them by many authors, including me. I will not add further to the somewhat blurred picture, except to say that now, after all the times I've encounterd them and all the attempts I've made to snare the trout they attract, I am quite happy today to stick to a tiny Red Tag. I have a number of patterns

'Stationary in flowless water'

which I must say do look more like the natural, but if the little Red Tag can be dropped with restrained force right on a feeding fish's nose such an approach is often irresistible. Some say the Red Tag imitates a beetle. Well, I have never seen a beetle that looks anything like one and neither have the trout, but due to its consistent all-season success and also the fact that it is taken dead drift, even stationary in flowless water, in my view, it simply appeals as a form of insect life worth a try.

Noel Jetson's Black Spinner has my total approval. I have heard the criticism that the long tails break off too easily when tying the fly on, but my answer is instant and severe. Just take care, that's all, it's your own fault if you break them. The thing is that the long tails work both as a rider to the fly and a bunch of carrots to the fish. In addition his proportions are right and the gold rib is better than silver. I use size 12 and 14. This is no nondescript but as close as you'll get in size and shape to the natural insect. A life fly.

Barry Lodge's Q-dun is an excellent imitation of the natural. Apart from size the chief requirement of any artificial representing the dun of our red spinner, black spinner, highland spinner, penstock brown or large black spinner is the single opaque wing which is conspicuous and instantly identifies it. Also it gives to it that essential yacht-like appearance. Not only has Barry achieved this but the colour and more importantly the proportions of his fly are excellent. What more can I say?

As for Max Christensen's Macquarie Red, I have devoted several pages to it in *The Way of an Angler* and cannot add further. But like many original designs, once the commercial fly-makers get going, short cuts are taken and substitutes used. Max's flies were tied on size 13 fine wire long-shanked mayfly hooks with a definite sneck bend which he imported from England. On any other hook they lose their original appearance and, for those few of us who are still around, who can tell at a glance one of Max's flies, they look a poor second rate. Max's tie sat up beautifully on the water and was a champion floater. I still have several unused which I keep aside, using old battered veterans or other similar flies tied by friends which follow his original design closely. But it was the special hook he used that gave the fly such a classic and unique look. It certainly fools the trout, often when other ties fail, and it must be classed as a life fly.

The small Dark Alder I find a good lifelike pattern. It gets results throughout the whole season and if restricted to its use alone one would do well. But in addition to the small size 14 and 16, I would like one or two short-shanked size 12. Early in the spring before the arrival of any kind of mayflies, on still mild middays there are sometimes sufficient numbers of small diptera rather like houseflies and a small Dark Alder is taken well, while in mid-summer the longer tie is a good nondescript especially on faster ripply streams. Its only drawback is its tendency to become difficult to follow where the water is shaded. Of added value is its effectiveness, often when midges are hatching.

For forty years I have used grasshopper flies, beginning with Gillie's Yellow Hopper. Then came O'Brien's, Birchdolt's, Hardy's, Ogden Smith's, Noel's Nobby, the original Nobby Hopper plus an odd pattern that somebody had

'Faster ripply streams'

given me. But several years ago a friend turned up with a box full of red-legged deer-hair and turkey-winged flies that just shouted success. I am unsure of the dressing's origin but think it came from South Africa. Most grasshopper flies look vaguely like a natural and rely on a lifelike presentation by landing them hard on the surface and then twitching towards you, success being mostly due to the way they are fished. But this fly looks more like a natural grasshopper than anything I've ever seen, so much so that I have many times had it taken dead drift or stationary. They come in sizes 12 and 10 and I use both.

The Senator's Choice was designed by Max Christensen and named after General R.H. Wordsworth who was at that time a member of the Australian Senate. It represents the orange-bodied sedge that frequents our upland lakes and streams in early summer and is most successful. However as a sedge imitation I'm not greatly impressed with it and I told Max so! In my opinion its sucess is due to its lifelike appearance, whatever it may resemble. This view is supported by the enthusiasm the trout show towards it on lowland streams when no sedges anything like it are ever seen. Max also tied the same fly with an olive body but it never had the same appeal either to me or the trout.

Now why on earth, you may say, does he include an Iron Blue Dun? Well, let me say first of all that my introduction to the fly took place in Britain, where from Scotland to southern England it got results regularly. Indeed, last time I was there I rarely used anything else—and I wasn't influenced by Plunket Greene. Mind you, I'm talking about the tie with the blue-grey body and red butt, not any of the variations. Secondly, here in Tasmania when the small black spinner *Atalonella delicatula* makes its first appearance in late September, this fly in size 14 is on its own when the duns begin and is often the fly on which I take my first trout for the year using the dry fly. Unfortunately it's not easy to obtain here, because it's not in common use. It's a life fly.

As for a small Black Ant, it's a must. Not that you'll need it all season. No, but as autumn approaches and, after rain, there comes a calm mild spell, out they come in millions in winged form, getting all over you and everything else including the river. They are only some three millimetres in length and a trout must consume a great number to obtain a good meal but take them they do with relish. Now, if you haven't got a tiny, say, size 16 imitation you're in trouble. You might undo one or two on this or that, but your refusals will be many. Frank Bond's tie is good; I like the little wings made from split jungle cock eye and the little bulbous bottom. It's hard to see at long range but strike at the rise and frequently you find yourself playing a fish. Another life fly.

The Hare's Ear and Gold ought to be more popular than it is. It's an excellent nondescript and just about unsinkable. There was a time when I used it as

'So it was one balmy afternoon'

much as a Red Tag. In the 1950s during the last years of the Shannon Rise I used it there successfully. But my reason for always having one with me in size 14 anyway, is because of an unforgettable failure and triumph I had a couple of years ago. Every autumn, whenever conditions are suitable, millions of little grey spiders float off across the fields carried by a thread of web which seems almost lighter than air; this is commonly referred to as ballooning. If you've not already experienced this happening it's quite a spectacle, the whole earth appearing to be covered by little drifting spiders. And into the river they go which pleases the trout no end, but unless you possess a fly of this pattern they will not please you. A Hardy's Favourite would do, you say, or a March Brown, or even a winged Hare's Ear. But believe me they will not do. No, there the trout are rising slowly and steadily, taking each spider with a gentle confidence, cruising around just under the surface so that you can see their aloof look as they reject your offering. So it was one balmy afternoon when I was totally vanquished. Pondering afterwards, however, I thought of the Hare's Ear and Gold, which I had left out of my boxes. How sweet was my success next day when, in similar weather, the spiders were again ballooning. And how the trout's smug faces changed as the little fly took hold. It would have to be called a life fly this time because they took it so slowly with such complete confidence.

The floating nymph is a pretty reliable standby not only on stillwaters when duns are being taken or appear to be, and all your best dun floaters are spurned, when in actual fact it is the nymph that is being eaten as it struggles at the surface to transform into the subimago. Once again you can see I'm being shrewd; I just don't like to get caught, that's all. Goodness knows the times when there is ample opportunity to have some sport are rare enough these days. Any kind of nymph can be made as a floater by the addition of side hackles so that it floats in or on the water's skin. They aren't too easy to see, but with a good idea where it is, you strike at the rise. I don't use the fly very often.

And finally Dick Woodard's Dragonfly. Everyone tears their hair out over dragonfly feeders. But not Dick, nor me either. Indeed I welcome them. I don't mean oncers, they're beyond us all. No, I mean those consistent leapers that pound up and down beside a weedbed leaping out every ten seconds or maybe a bit more. This is a definite lifelike technique, and unless the fly is fished correctly it is no more use than a gum leaf. First you must get in step with the fish, know exactly his beat and travel, then cast quickly and accurately, dropping the fly, often tail first, right on his track, when, if it is not snatched even before it hits the water or shortly afterwards, you lift off and wait for the next chance. No good comes from leaving it there dead drift, although I admit I have occasionally had it taken this way.

As for the complicated tie; I gave this in Dick's own words in *Ripples, Runs and Rises* and it must be followed precisely. So much time is needed to make one fly that commercial dressing is unlikely. Should I get hooked up using Dick's fly I go to extraordinary lengths to retrieve it. This is totally a lifelike fly.

So there we are, twelve assorted floaters and a heap left on the table. Oh, I can hear the questions and exclamations. Why hasn't he got a Greenwell or Royal Coachman, or Cock-y-bondu or whatever? Well, if you'll be quiet for a minute, I've picked out twelve different patterns for twelve different circumstances. The best twelve. Of course I carry a Greenwell, Wickam, or Cocky or Royal and others. I picked out only what I thought gave me a good chance in the situations I speak of. Certainly carry the usual favourites, but if it came to a limit of twelve essentials, this is my list.

When last I was in Scotland I purchased one of those Wheatley aluminium fly boxes for wet flies that has a folding leaf or flap in the centre so that there are four separate panels of flies with individual spring clips—all very neat and convenient. Starting at the top of one side of the centre flap is a row of eight Peter Ross, below this a row of Furnace Brown, then Greenwells, Jock Scott, Butcher, Mallard and Claret, Mrs Simpson and Black Pennel. On the other side it's Watson's Fancy, Alexandra, Zulu and Kingfisher, Invicta, Bloody Mary and Watsons Mate, Woolly Worm and Peacock & Black.

The other panels with bigger clips contain, on one side, a mixture of larger wets including Yeti, Muddler Minnow and a variety of matukas, even Yellow Peril and Whitebait. The other side has a wide range of Robins, Hairy Mary, Streamers and Bucktails. As you can see I have a pretty comprehensive boxful, but not one of them is a life fly, they are either lifelike or just plain exciters. All the sea trout flies like Peter Ross and Watson's Fancy are fished in a lifelike manner twitched, jiggled and tumbled. The Robins and Streamers are retrieved faster appealing to the trout's pugnacity as something worth chasing and catching. They represent nothing. In another aluminium case is a collection of nymphs, scud, snails, caddis sticks and bugs, which, together with ways they are fished, I will talk about in a later chapter.

That's my subaqueous ammunition.

Thinking back over the past, I recall two very clear occasions when the old much discussed and widely accepted theory that the key to success lies in matching the hatch was completely shot to pieces. For this to happen it is necessary to have many anglers fishing simultaneously at the same place. Firstly I refer to the Shannon Rise here in Tasmania with thousands of snowflake caddis hatching with umpteen anglers on the river. Many a time six or more rods would take fish by differing methods on different flies at the same time. Why would one angler take trout on a floating sedge while another a few yards away succeeded using a Red Tag? Or a Brown Nymph? My conclusion is that they were both fishing their chosen fly properly in a lifelike manner. Pattern was irrelevant.

Secondly, I remember Lake King William in its early days when the population of phreatoicids, or scud, was enormous, the decaying vegetation and detritus apparently being ideal for their explosive increase. The trout were in the shallows grubbing about feasting on these semi-blind little crustaceans. I had great success with a plain dark green matuka, taking bag limits each day. But others were either not successful at all, or only partly so. Many also used matukas, while others fished a wide assortment of flies. I am absolutely certain that it was not the pattern that mattered, but the lifelike manner in which I fished it. Even longtime anglers like Jos Sculthorpe and Bre Lutwytche struggled to take fish.

Now, there they all were, first at the Shannon Rise then at Lake King William, fishing dry and wet flies galore, some succeeding and some not. I am convinced that, in the former case, it was essential to have a drag-free drift—not an easy thing in such swirling cross-currented water—requiring skilled, accurate, snaky casting ability which is not given to many. In the second case the matuka had to be worked with a fast, jerky action to attract the attention of the bottom-feeding fish. Next time you meet someone enjoying success, rather than enquire what fly he is using, ask him about the speed and action with which he is working his fly. Watch him, and the dry fly man also, and note how he overcomes drag. In both cases it's the lifelike appearance of the fly that is important and the confidence you have in a particular pattern. As Joe Brooks said, 'To fish without confidence is not to fish at all'. Consider some of the great anglers; Oliver Kite managed with about four dry flies only, Harry Plunket Greene with just the Iron Blue Dun, John Waller Hills used a Caperer more than anything else. Locally Dick Wigram mostly used a Black Spinner or Brown Nymph, Reg Clayton a Red Tag, Fred Stewart a Royal Coachman, Geoff Hall and Black Beetle. Others enjoyed season after season with a very limited box of artificials in varying sizes.

So entomology doesn't count? Well, let's face it, so far as actual fishing goes it really doesn't. It's more a matter of basic size and shape rather than tackle or wing colour. Take some of the favourites like Greenwell's Glory, Tups and Firey Brown or Watson's Fancy, Butcher and Alexandra. What do they represent? Nothing. But as an adjunct to fishing, as a fascinating study of the

'Swirling cross-currented water'

trout's natural food, its life cycle and habitat needs, entomology is of tremendous value and interest. All the great anglers I've ever known have had a keen interest in the life and times of the natural models upon which the art is based. Numbers of fishermen aren't interested and as their total increases the general entomological knowledge of the fly-fishing world decreases. I wonder if things will change?

3 Seeing Is Believing

For some time I have not been completely convinced about the various theories offered over many years by numerous writers concerning how and what a trout sees. But not any more. Let me tell you now that most of it is inaccurate and misleading. All that I am about to say is based on careful experimentation plus close observation and can be verified by witnesses. I simply ask you to put aside all you have read or heard on the subject and hear me out.

I am aware that to understand the trout's visual system a comparison with the human eye is helpful and requires a knowledge of how light moves through different mediums and how it is refracted. I realise that an anatomical comparison is necessary with suitable explanation regarding the differences and how each system operates. But I prefer first to tell you about my experiments and then offer some scientific explanation.

I first became interested in and soon fascinated with a trout's visual ability when I began flipping grasshoppers out to cruising fish in my dam at home. My interest increased rapidly, especially when I found 'Go-Cat' pellets just as acceptable to the trout as grasshoppers and requiring no catching. This star-shaped cat food is slightly less in size than your little fingertail, comes in several insect-like colours, floats and rather resembles a beetle or similar terrestrial insect. So I had an abundant supply of food and, wearing polaroid glasses on sunny days, I began a serious study of the subject.

The trout in my dam are mostly rainbows but this is irrelevant; their feeding behaviour is the same as for brown trout. Having successfully gained the attention of one fish it was not long before another would join the first to rise to this 'hatch of beetles'. Soon a third would come and after perhaps half an hour as many as four or five trout were within three metres of me so long as I remained still. They were happy to rise to order.

At first, when there was only one fish present, I was interested to see from how far away it would be aware of a pellet's arrival on the water's surface. This I found to be about two metres and it was obvious that it was the disturbance of the surface that attracted it. But when there were several trout nearby they all saw the pellet drop in and all rushed to it simultaneously to get to it first. The resultant mêlée caused the surface to be ruffled violently as they jostled each other for the 'beetles'. I then tossed out perhaps half a dozen pellets together which caused the water to literally boil. I threw several more and it would have been at this point that I realised that the trout, in spite of the commotion, must actually have been able to see the pellets they fought after. And this meant only one thing: that all the theories concerning the trout's vision that I had read—about windows, refraction, mirrors and so on—were invalid.

So, forgetting about tossing a pellet at various distances in front of a fish so it could see it hit the surface, I began a series of experiments waiting until there were no trout nearby then flicking a single pellet out to watch what happened. The surface for all these experiments was smooth and the inquiry now became quite complex, involving the depth of the trout, its forward vision, its peripheral vision and its visual acuity at different distances from the floating food. These studies were all carried out under calm, sunny conditions over about two months. My conclusions and some further details regarding these features are as follows.

The maximum and minimum depth of the fish varied from five to forty centimetres and I will specify this as each topic is considered. It is clear that the trout's forward binocular vision covers some forty degrees and is slightly overlapped by its monocular peripheral vision which extends all the way around to the blind spot at the rear with acuity reducing towards this point. This blind area occupies about the same angle as its forward biniocular vision. The other blind spots are directly below, just above its head and immediately in front of its snout. Binocular vision, I should explain, is the ability of the brain to take visual information from two eyes to form a single image.

A trout has an extensive area of peripheral vision occupying at least one hundred and fifty degrees both upwards and downwards and sideways which will be considered in detail shortly. And it is also clear that the regions of greatest acuity overlap forward and above the snout, giving it a long narrow arc where its binocular vision is best and sharpest.

Now, after intently observing my single floating pellet, I can confidently report the following: First that, as with humans, the trout has an area of conscious awareness in its most developed field of gaze looking directly ahead. Time and again I watched and, so long as the fish approached the floating pellet directly towards it, the food was seen and taken. There are two aspects that must be

'Approached the floating pellet directly towards it'

mentioned also. One, that the average depth at which a fish had obviously become aware of the pellet would be thirty-five centimetres and the average distance forty, but there were just as many occasions when the trout passed by on either side of the pellet without being aware of it.

This is a clear illustration of unconscious vision, which is the same with you and I. As a demonstration I would ask you now to fix your eyes on an object about three or four metres away and extend your arms at full stretch sideways. Now, with your gaze firmly fixed on the object, notice that your hands are hardly apparent at all and certainly not in your conscious vision. Now suddenly twiddle the fingers of one hand. It will immediately catch your eye. Then try the other side.

To prove my theory I held a long thin stick out like a fly rod, quite stationary, until a fish came slowly by unaware of the pellet to one side. When it was level with the food, or beam on, I poked the pellet to make it move slightly. At once the trout noticed, turned and took it. Next, in attempting to establish the depth/distance ratio, I waited until I had a couple of fish by themselves and excited them with occasional well-placed pellets. By this means I got one so close to the edge that it was in no more than fifteen centimetres of water. But at a range of say twenty centimetres it could still see the pellet on the surface.

Next, I placed a single pellet on a flat stone at the edge and gently pushed it off onto the water so that it floated slowly out to where the depth would only have been about ten centimetres. If it drifted closer to shore I pushed it out again with the stick. Several trout passed by in both directions at range varying from half to a metre or more, but as it was in their peripheral vision, none saw it. At length a single trout came directly towards it and very clearly at a distance of say half a metre saw the pellet, accelerated, and rose to it.

I repeated this exercise many times demonstrating it to my wife and at least one other witness. I have no doubt whatever that a fish at a depth of say ten centimetres can see a food item like this on the surface at a distance of fifty centimetres. On one occasion, however—and this I found a real surprise— there was a fitful breeze that came and went with long calm periods between blows. Having pushed my pellet out on the calm surface as usual I suddenly found it being blown sideways by quite a ripple which became almost little wavelets. Thus it approached a small flat stone that protruded a couple of centimetres above the surface and there, on its top, my pellet was washed and left high and dry. Soon the next calm period came, and I care not about your belief or disbelief, for the first trout that saw it recognised it as food and, showing a fair portion of its body, grasped it from the rock surface!

But I am not finished with my account yet. Not by any means. I have long

'Turned and took it'

marvelled at the remarkable agility and ability of trout leaping from the water to take airborne dragonflies, damselflies and mayflies. I have spent some time watching them from an elevated position as, in the case of the former, they actually track the prey, waiting for it to hesitate stationary for a few moments, a half metre or more above the surface, before flinging themselves out to seize it in midair. This activity must surely cause the window theorists to think, in an effort to provide an explanation. Not only can the trout see up through the water out into the air with great acuity, but then, leaping from one medium to the other, rapidly reducing the distance between itself and the insect, using its binocular vision with remarkable accuracy, grasps it and falls back into the water.

Thinking about this, I cut the barb off a Black Spinner dry fly and using my eleven-foot graphite rod, dangled it out over the water and waited for a fish to approach, allowing the fly to simply hang motionless about forty centimetres above the surface. My arms became tired so I propped the rod on a forked stick and just watched. At length a trout came by and in due course another but neither took the slightest notice of the fly. Both had been slightly to one side so, thinking that peripheral vision may have been involved, I waited until another fish swam directly beneath the fly. Again it did not appear to notice the fly but after a few minutes it returned in the opposite direction. This time I jiggled the fly up and down rather like a natural insect. The response was immediate. At a distance of some thirty-five centimetres it rushed forward to leap at the fly, grasping it firmly for a few moments before it pulled free as the trout splashed back into the water.

The conclusion was obvious: until the fly was agitated it was not in the fish's conscious vision as it looked directly ahead. As before I repeated this experiment several times with similar results. But when I gave a to and fro pendulum-like motion to the fly it did not appear to be as noticeable to the trout, and was more difficult for it to grasp. But if, at any time, I allowed the fly to drop to the surface for an instant, thereby creating a ring, the fish was immediately conscious of it and at a far greater range. Applying this observation to fishing when airborne insects are being taken by trout and they are becoming very difficult to catch because their conscious vision is locked into searching only for individuals above the surface, a fly which can be dropped a little more heavily on the water than normal, just at the right moment for the fish to see it land, has much more chance of success than a floating fly.

It will be of interest now to compare the trout's eye with that of humans. There are a number of similarities. Both have a cornea and lens to direct light, a retina to perceive light and an optic nerve to transfer visual information to the brain. The trout, however, lacks protective eyelids and since its eyes are located laterally along the side of its head it possesses extensive peripheral vision. In order for the human eye to focus on both near and far objects, the lens changes shape to increase or decrease its power. In contrast, the lens of a trout does not change shape but instead moves in a plane forwards and backwards to focus an image on the back of the eye. The trout has coordinated eye movement by the use of muscles attached to the onside of each eye giving it ocular motion comparable to that of humans. Whereas the lens of the human eye is oval in shape, that of the trout is so powerful that it is roughly spherical. Thus when it views distant objects everything from approximately two metres and beyond is in focus on the retina at the same time. As you and I reach the age of forty-five or so our lens loses much of its ability to change shape and hence the need for reading glasses for close work. The trout has no such problem throughout its life.

Scientists tell us that the trout's vision is inferior to that of humans and that not until it views something at a distance of about eight centimetres is it able to see in detail. Although we may surpass the trout in visual acuity, the trout has a much larger area of visual surveillance and is better adapted for seeing at night. But I believe what I see, and when I observe a trout leaping out of the water to grasp a flying insect I am persuaded that its sight is far from poor at a distance of say half a metre. And this applies to objects below the surface, on it, or above it.

And that's that.

4 Success and Failure

Goodness knows how many successes and failures I've had since those first wonderful days of youth when I strode over the paddocks like a hare, waded the roughest rock-strewn rapids with ease, clambered over logs like an ant, tied knots with ridiculous simplicity, bounded over fences like a deer and basked in the warm sunshine like a lizard. But I do not intend boring you with numerous tales of yore. No. Two will do. One of each. So, in accordance with the chapter heading, I will take success first. I'm no Plunket Greene or John Hills, but will do my best.

During summer the trout in the St Patricks River, as in most streams, tend to lie in shady corners where there is little flow, leisurely sucking down any hapless creature that floats their way. Their rises are often silent or accompanied by that delicious sound, quite unique in all the world, which any old-time stream-fisher will immediately detect and which is guaranteed to stop him in his tracks, eyes straining and ears alert for a repeat performance. One becomes conditioned to this sound; many times I have been out with non-fisher friends or beginners, and they are just not conscious of it. Even when you try to direct them, if it's a gentle rise they still might miss it.

But Noel, the angler friend I had with me this day, is well schooled in the ways of the wiliest stream trout, finding a special delight in hard-to-get-at fish. Indeed the more difficult they are the more enthusiastic he is. The numbers fisher, of course, knows nothing of this and walks past, even if he's aware of the trout's location. For him it's just too hard; just not possible. For him the kill element exceeds the skill element.

Somewhere about mid-morning we came to an ideal righthand bend, shallow on our side with a pebbly bottom, a wall of tall tea-trees behind, while the far side was deep, dark and almost flowless. A large dead tree lay in the stream, its bare branches making a sort of screen between the two sides. And then it

'The St Patrick's River'

happened, the faintest sip and tiny ring of a rise, far across beneath the opposite bank overhung by blackwoods and brush. Then, in a few moments, another sipping rise, clearly made by an above-average fish for the St Pats. 'There y'are,' declared Noel. 'Go on, have a go.'

Silently I surveyed the situation. At first glance it looked quite impossible. But no, there was a chance—the merest chance—to fire a shot between two branches forming a vee, with about a metre of space in total. With my favourite righthand sidecast I could have done it all easily, but there was no room behind for that; an overhead steeple cast was the only answer. Nothing ventured nothing gained, the worst that could happen would be a lost fly and dented self-image. No, worse still would be the glance of derision from my speckled friend who knew all about me and considered himself safe. Even worse still would be to have moved on without an attempt.

But even if I did manage to get him on, I now thought about my chances of getting him out. The screen of branches divided us at all points except at the narrow vee near its centre, the trout on the far side tempting me and Noel on my left side goading me. There was no way out now so concentrating like mad, when you forget the whole world, I made several false casts to get the range and take aim, before making the one and only cast possible since there was no way at all of retrieving for another.

Sometimes, just sometimes, things go perfectly, and thus with much fortune did things go now. Not a word passed between us as the small Royal Coachman drifted towards the mark. You could hardly have asked for a better coverage; in under the overhanging bush the fly fell, as if propelled by magic, not too far over, not too far short and just a nice distance ahead. So far so good.

Next came the rise, not hesitant but deliberate and confident. Still not a word was spoken. Then whoa! Halt! Have done! My strike brought instant action, the quiet pool shattered by a splashing pounder as I held him tight near the surface. I had learnt before that the only way to get a fish over or through a weedbed is to manhandle it, taking the chance of loss. It helps, however, to wait until it is heading towards you and then just try to keep it coming, its wriggling and twisting often assisting by parting the weeds. These were my tactics now, at the first opportunity, as he flung himself clear of the water, to land still wildly thrashing on my side of the obstacles. The rest was easy and requires no explanation. 'There y'are,' I said. 'Yep, there y'are,' replied Noel.

I have a vast collection of failures from which to choose. But there are failures and failures. Even a bad failure is not so bad if followed by a success. And the greater the success the less the failure. The reverse is not as good because

'Low water levels'

you finish the day with an unpleasant feeling instead of the glow of satisfaction. Undoubtedly the worst scenario is a series of failures, but this is rare—if the chances come you're pretty sure to make some sort of score. There is, however, another situation that can only be described as devastating. And it's this woeful subject I propose to talk about now.

In mid-summer the dog days descend on us with a consistency that never deserts them. Sometimes they are accompanied by a steady wind from the northwest which makes the flat mayfly streams a completely hopeless proposition while things might not be much better on the broken streams descending from the mountains. High air temperature, lack of flylife and low water levels all combine to produce this gloomy time, the only activity occurring at dawn and dusk when the wind is absent. There are days, however, when it begins after breakfast and slowly increases to a steady blow by midday which it maintains until well after dark. Maybe you can find some grasshopper fishing where there is enough cool deep flow. I hope you do.

Every now and then, however, you get a calmer and milder day, perhaps with the gentlest of southwesterlies when it's a pleasure to be out. The sun shines, but is not hot enough to burn your skin, or produce that shimmering bright glare that makes a hat and sunglasses essential. In weather like this a few trout might well be found browsing about in search of food. On such a day I was myself searching along a South Esk billabong, but found no trout doing likewise. Not a fish moved anywhere and I polaroided acres of blank water. There I sat at the end of the billabong in the shade of a lone willow enjoying my freshly made tomato sandwiches, grapes, cucumber and celery. A chilled glass of white wine was all I needed. No, it was not. I needed to see a rise! And what sort of story would this be without one? But far away near the right hand side I saw it. Only once and I rivetted my gaze on the spot. He rose again, coming my way. What an extraordinary sport we have!

Away went the sandwiches and away went I. Making a detour I approached the bank slowly polaroiding carefully and ready for action. For over two hours I had scanned this long pool without the faintest sign of a trout yet here he was simply appearing out of the blue. Now I could see him. He had been further along the edge but was returning, about two metres out, half a metre beneath the surface and swimming quite steadily. I froze. About a cricket pitch away he rose again followed by another a few metres on. But what was he taking? I could see nothing on the surface. Now he was heading away again and at the very extremity of the pool he rose once more and I rather feared this would be his last. But presently there was another ring, this time somewhat closer. Delighted with my good fortune, I waited eagerly as he retraced his track towards me, rising gently about every ten metres. The size and form of the rise resembled that of a caenid take, but there were no caenids. I reasoned the only thing possible were a few tiny lerp insects, like miniature cicadas, fallen from the tussocks. I waited all ready. Here he comes. I can see him plainly. Pale ochre green. Now he's very clear, and very close.

Follow me carefully and decide where I went wrong. I dared not cast as he approached. Instead I froze again until he had passed and, I would estimate at a range of eight metres, making just one backcast, dropped the number 14 Red Tag a half metre to the left and a metre ahead. Instantly he changed course, came straight to it and rose nicely. I paused and then struck. Nothing! At first I couldn't believe it, everything seemed perfectly in order. He appeared to have risen faultlessly and taken the fly well. Then came a flood of disappointment, annoyance and a black mark against my ability. I had botched it and was angry with myself, the whole sad performance growing steadily worse as the afternoon passed, until finally having not set eyes on another trout, I left the billabong under a black cloud of dismay, completely defeated. Down but not out, because I shall return.

5 Ways and Means

There are many methods by which trout may be caught. Indeed, using bait of some kind, they are the easiest of fish to take, far simpler they tell me, than tench, carp or dace. Grayling too are said to be hard to catch at times using bait. At an early age I used to be taken out by several bait fishers using worms. These outings I enjoyed, but one particular man showed me how to use an oyster as bait, which was a most successful method. He carried several unopened in his bag and, once in his chosen position, tied the freshly opened oyster onto a bream hook using strong white cotton to make a little parcel of it. Not only did it seem irresistible to the trout, but unless you got snagged and lost it, the one bait lasted for up to a day's fishing because, being tied together, it did not come apart in the trout's mouth and once unhooked was all ready for further use.

Some of my first attempts to catch trout were by means of an oyster like this. I also tried worms, but not often. Blackfishing provided much happiness. On warm summer evenings, perched on a log in a deep snaggy corner I would lower my worm into the dark water with all the skill I possessed, landing maybe eight or ten nice blackfish before the eels came on the bite, when I'd go home. Other baits I sometimes tried were grasshoppers and cockchafer beetles, these being coated with 'Cerolene' to make them float better and thereby entice the trout to the surface to take them. I'm sure this was the catalyst that directed me towards dry-fly fishing, which, once witnessed in practice, has captivated me to this day.

Also when I was a small boy I was taken out trolling a number of times by a dentist at Eildon Weir in Victoria. This method I also tried alone, rowing a wooden dinghy for kilometres around the lake, using two rods at the same time. Hand spinning I tried, before the advent of today's fixed spool reel, when

'A deep snaggy corner'

the spinner was cast little more than twice the rod's length and retrieved by hand. This took place almost entirely on streams but very occasionally I tried the technique at Eildon Weir of casting from a boat close to shore. In the 1930s I graduated to trials with the first threadline fixed-spool reels produced. The line was of braided silk and quite strong. Crochet cotton was also used, but not very successfully because it tended to untwist and tangle. A devon spinner was chiefly employed, or an eelskin with treble hooks with sometimes a feather at the tail. At this stage the wonders of fly-fishing were unknown to me, but my learning about streamcraft and the ways of trout was progressing steadily. This fundamental grounding is missed by today's instant experts who begin their fishing by means of the fly with only a crude and superficial knowledge of the sport. So they are inclined to make a lot of noise and ill-informed comments.

But long before I left school I was quite a proficient stream fly-fisher, making my own flies and already studying the life cycles of trout foods. My school holidays were always spent fishing. And, looking back, comparing my ability then to that of today's so-called experts, without being boastful, I could have taught them a thing or two even then. I was self-educated as an angler, learning from books and experience. So before World War II began I was well versed in most methods of trout angling, fished using the fly alone, and was able to enjoy my fishing on some of the world's famous streams while serving overseas in the air force.

As a fly-fisher, then, with a fair idea of what it's all about, before going further, you must know that you're dealing with a dry-fly crank, so before talking about subaqueous approaches I will fire off a few warning shots to make myself clear. Lord Harmsworth, for a start, says 'Truly the dry-fly fisherman is wiser than others.' Halford loved to angle for 'fish indulging in the legitimate pursuit of the floating fly.' John Turnbull makes things quite plain, 'But to all true anglers dry-fly fishing is the method which really brings delight.' And John Roberts sums up saying, 'However, my greatest pleasure of all the different techniques and tactics for brown and rainbow trout is to fish with a floating fly.' And without even a word from Walker, Hills, Gordon or Plunket Greene, Vincent Marinaro is invincible, 'Let personal preference, *sans peur, sans reproche*, determine the choice. Mine is the dry fly.' And so is mine.

There are times, however, when the dry fly is a lost cause. In early season, for instance, when it's cold, wind, rain and floods, or at any time during rough weather the floater is a loser. What then? For me it's the wet fly which I find both fascinating and demanding considerable skill and knowledge. It's active with sometimes boisterous results when a fish takes. In other words I'm an

'During rough weather'

either or angler—either dry or wet. Note I do not even mention nymph fishing, because I can't abide it. As one writer puts it, 'I can't see what's happening.' And another, after trying unsuccessfully with the dry fly, 'No doubt a nymph was the proper fare for him.' And another, 'when many other flies have failed.' Stephen Rider Haggard puts it, 'I always feel a twinge of guilt. Perhaps all fly-fishers are Catholics at heart—we like to bend our personal rules a bit, but we always confess it afterwards. Fish caught on a dry-fly always seem more valuable than those taken on a nymph.'

I will go further. I cannot see much difference really between using an upstream floating worm and nymph fishing. In the latter case casting is far simpler. Unlike a worm the artificial cannot be easily dislodged from the hook. Also I do not care for the bright almost gaudy strike indicators which are these days added to the leader, making it all look a bit like a fancy dress. The upstream and drift down approach using a nymph has something, I suppose, if you must. But it's a second-rate operation and its fisher is described by one commentator as an 'unhandy practitioner in the supremest of the Arts.'

But far worse is the weighted nymph which is allowed to sink to the bottom to bounce amongst the stones, the whole procedure only separated from bait fishing on the bottom by the fact that the bait is artificial. Nymph fishing at night is bordering on the abject and as Halford says, those who descend to it should 'agree to abstain for the future from this most undesirable practice.' Another comment claims that nymph fishers of any ilk are to be included in the category of those whose 'great ambition of life in any department of the sport is to beat their own or other people's records.' I don't know that I would go as far as this but like Halford I am not in favour of night fishing. I know they fish for sea trout in Britain like this but I'm not in favour of that either.

Some of my oldest angling friends use nymphs. And what's more some have been fishing for many years in many places. I do not quite understand this so remain like Marinaro, concluding that it's each to his own. Laurence Catlow, paying tribute to the finest fly-fisherman he ever knew writes, 'He loved the dry-fly and, by the time he was sixty, he felt no need for any other fishing style. His purism was of the generous and informed sort: an individual preference which left others to do as they wanted.'

It does bother me, however, to see a noble trout rising gracefully, totally defeating an angler using a floater, then to be rudely extracted when the angler resorts to a nymph, the whole scene becoming clouded and tending towards the underhand, certainly mildewed. So be it. Now don't talk to me about Skues, Sawyer or Wigram. It's all been done to death and only makes things unpleasant as I contemplate a calm, mild morning and the trout rising freely.

How do you tell an old hand from the ordinary, a listener from a talker, a true angler from a numbers fisher? Watch him, that's all, just watch him. He approaches the pool like a panther. From exactly the right angle he casts with a fast action and high backcast. Except for his arm there is no movement in his slightly forward stance. Between casts the rod comes back only once. It's lift off, backcast—shortening or lengthening—and forward all in the one action. If the fly needs drying it's done with a whip-crack cast away from the target. Dick Wigram was an excellent caster. I always thought his stance heron-like, his body not moving at all. He still remains the only caster I have ever seen able to lift off from a long distance and, in one action—that is once back and once forward—cover a rise close to him, either in front or to one side. Fred Stewart, on the other hand, was not a good caster; he got his fly where he wanted it by sheer persistence. Quick arrow-like casts were not his forte. But both these past champions had superb streamcraft and trout knowledge.

Lake fishers don't have to be good casters. Distance is important to them so they really need to be able to double-haul. But the sidecast is rarely if ever needed, nor the spey, or the several anti-drag casts. The backhand sidecast is, of course, unheard of. But this is essential to the stream angler and, at the risk of repeating myself because I think I must have mentioned it in some previous writing, be advised by the finest backhand sidecaster who ever was, Reg Clayton. 'Point the reel directly at the spot where your fly must go,' he would tell you, and the rest of your problems, such as clearing obstacles, are easily overcome. This is because your wrist is turned sideways; it is quite impossible to sidecast with the reel facing downwards. It was wonderful to watch Reg in action and I shall ever be thankful to have had such a fishing companion—a gentle, God-fearing man with the driest yet most effervescent humour.

'Never leave rising fish,' Reg sometimes declared. And he was right. You must have done it. I know I have. There you are with several risers to occupy you, but what do you do? 'Oh,' you say to yourself, 'judging by what's on here, I reckon they'd really be going further up.' So off you go as fast as you can, cutting off the next bend to get there sooner, only to find that they are not going at all, so back you come to find they've stopped where you should have stayed. Why they have ceased rising, of course, is that the wind has arrived or strengthened. And once I mention my arch enemy I'm suddenly reminded of the words of the Reverend Richard Durnford and how he too must have been plagued. Wind was always the first item mentioned in his detailed diary: for example, very calm, too slack, insufficient, sufficient, quite sufficient, moderate, brisk, fierce, whistling, strong, violent and hurricane. I know how to describe it and it doesn't bare printing. Anyway, getting back to never leaving a rising fish, 'It's all very well for you to give advice,' you say. Well I'm not. It's coming to you from Reg Clayton. What an angler.

You'll sometimes hear somebody say, 'I can't fish from a boat,' meaning he doesn't like it. But if he only knew how to boat-fish and had become adept at it, he'd like it I'm sure. Reg and I fished the lakes from a boat during the dog days of summer, when the streams are low, possessing that look of burnished steel with not a rise to be seen anywhere. We fished both dry and wet, sometimes with great success. And, yes, we found it both testing and rewarding. But how we looked forward to the cooler weather and a return to the streams.

But during the last decade or so the deep-sunk bottom style of numbers wet-fly fishing has crept into boat fishing at many lakes. I've done a fair amount of bream fishing from a boat, using prawns or pretty fish as bait. You toss out and let the sinker take you to the bottom. With a bit of a twitch now and then you wait for a bite and strike. It's good fun and can be most exciting. But this is no way to catch a trout! Yet the methods used by some so-called fly fishermen are remarkably similar. How pleased I have been at some places in America, England, Scotland, Wales and Switzerland to find this style of fishing disallowed and instead dry-fly fishing only. I have never heard of any water being restricted to nymph or wet-fly only.

I cannot think of boat-fishing without mention of the lochs of Scotland and fishing the Bloody Butcher and Black Pennel along the edges with a skilled boatman, or gillie, on the oars. He knew and you knew which way and where the boat should go. And you knew that he knew. This is what I call wet-fly fishing from a boat, working the little bays, weed beds, calms and ripples. Searching, not by chance but with knowledge borne of long experience and with skill; an intensely interesting and absorbing art, rewarded by a take or simply a 'Good cast, Sir' from the gillie. The Scottish summer evenings are long, as they can be anywhere in Britain. It's after tea that you depart, the air often still and warm. I've had great fishing in Wales, as I have at Penstock Lagoon in Tasmania when only a few anglers went there, with Reg at the paddles or vice versa. Boatmanship is half the battle—we would take it turn about, changing as one took a fish. It is important when fishing from a boat, especially when dealing with a large trout, to bring the fish to the net, not the reverse. Chasing the hooked fish around with an open net often ends with it breaking free under the boat or loss through a frightened charge. And don't stand up to do it either.

The Americans talk about percentage fishing. I'm not perfectly clear about what this means, but these days the fishing I enjoy most and naturally that which

'They have ceased rising'

I seek especially, is what I call percentage fishing. First the trout has to be visible. Either you polaroid him by searching, or else he discloses his whereabouts by rising and thereby becomes visible. Next you allow yourself just a single cast. If you then get one rise, make one strike then play and land the fish cleanly, that's one hundred per cent. Do it again, that's two hundred. And so on. But make one mistake and back you go to the start. It's like Snakes and Ladders and most enjoyable with an extra challenge. I find that to get a score of six hundred percent for the day is a good result. When conditions are suitable I declare it a 'percentage day'; needless to say this means dry-fly only.

I like best a cruiser rather than a riser in a fixed position. Being allowed only one shot you must judge it carefully. If you are off target he will not see your fly. If too close he is scared. Of course you may well place it perfectly only to have it ignored altogether, or given a glance or long cold examination before refusal. But a cruiser on patrol is so intriguing to watch; it's a cat and mouse situation. Sometimes he's at a distance, at others close as he meanders around a backwater or still pool. Many a time I've had a trout swim past right under my rod-tip, when you can see his every spot, the look in his eye, the grin or grimace, the arrogance or solemnity.

Now, when at very close range like this, should you so much as blink too conspicuously he'll spot you and depart in a huff. I have adopted a standard approach: rod held in right hand, leader in left just above the fly, a metre of slack from the reel, forefinger of right hand clamping line to cork handle. If Mr Speckles now comes sauntering by all I need do is fractionally part my left thumb and forefinger to let the fly pendulum out and down to land, all being well, right in front of his nose. I'm still only allowed one go like this—it counts as a cast in my percentage fishing.

For the past two seasons I have been made to look like Simple Simon by a collection of fish that patrol along the edge beneath a sheer, high clay bank opposite. It's too far to throw across so all I have thus far achieved is the laughter of this gang of six or so. They have treated me not only with scorn, but a nasty kind of ridicule. But no more! Oh no, I have found a way to get myself to the other side, so I can peep over the edge and secretly watch as they leer across on lookout for me. And then, ho ho, I will take up my attacking stance and wait my chance until an unsuspecting individual comes idling along, fins paddling gently, gliding slowly forward like oil, so confident and hauty. Down will drop my Red Tag, leaving a little ring as it alights. Seeing this he will make the worst blunder of his life, as I see the white mouth open and close. The strike will be vertical and solid. As Halford says: 'One must strike slowly because big fish rise slowly. One must strike with sufficient force to drive the hook home.'

'Discloses his whereabouts by rising'

I can only, with glee, imagine his reaction. For an instant it will simply be shock. Then embarrassment. Then anger, as he charges across the pool, leaping high and slashing frantically, the spray and bubbles flung wide. What a sight I'm in for and what a state of excitement. I can hardly wait!

6 Plant and Equipment

Writing in *Trout and Salmon* magazine Frank Murgett tells of fishing in Ireland, of when the angler from England is met by his gillie for the day named Henry O'Reilly, who, casting his pale blue eyes over the Englishman's tackle, comments, 'Ah, sor, 'tis yourself will be bringing the kitchen sink with you next.' And I can well imagine it; at least one tackle-dealer uses twleve or more consecutive pages to advertise his vast array of gear in this same publication. There's no doubting that fly-fishers have become equipment freaks and tackle junkies, the younger the fisher the more gadgets he acquires.

This is more understandable in Britain, where the post-war fly-fishing explosion has gathered many past bait-fishers to the fold whose offspring now follow in their parents' footsteps. Thus the great popularity of the sunk line and weird things adorning the hooks attached thereto is explained. Where once the bait was natural, it is now artificial. There is little other difference. The tackle-makers, of course, have seized the opportunity and produced a wide range of sinking lines and so on to suit this style of fishing. It gripes the old brigade to see this; it's a bit like a whiteman journalist writing a review of an Aboriginal's poems: he knows nothing of their feelings, culture or dreamtime. And nor does this bottom-fishing, nymph or fly-drowning chap know much about real fly-fishing, reducing this grand and unique surface-feeding fish to the level of a perch.

But the American angler, although rarely this kind of bottom-fisher, is nevertheless an irredeemable tackle gearhead. It's hard to contemplate, but at the 1991 Fly Tackle Dealer Show in Denver there were 365 booths displaying a staggering amount of gear. Manufacturers, distributors, fly-shop owners, leading anglers, tackle reps and the media all came to buy and sell, look and learn. Everything you could think of was there from the finest rods in the world

to plain gizmos and widgets. For two and a half nine-hour days it went on, the whole show done in typical American style. And yes, if I'd had the chance I'd have gone along for a look too. You must have seen some of those delightful caricatures of a fly-fisher standing proudly attired and bedangled with all manner of bits and pieces. If you don't need something then go without it and look less like a clown!

Let's start at the top. I dislike caps of any sort and that's that. On return from the war I had one myself given to me by an American pilot. But I soon found that it didn't protect my ears or the back of my neck, whereas hats protect everything. I don't, however, particularly like those wide-brimmed 'Aussie' hats. Polaroids are a must. If you buy a pair of very good but very expensive ones then hang them around your neck or else you will either sit on them, leave them behind somewhere or drop them over the side of a boat. I don't mind what shirt and trousers you choose so long as they're sombre in colour. A vest or fishing waistcoat is also a must. There are numerous makes; my present one comes from New Zealand with eight pockets in front, three zipped, and a large zipped one at the back. Those in front hold fly-boxes and so on, while that behind takes your lunch and a rolled up, light-weight waterproof coat.

Waders come in either chest or thigh length depending on whether you wade deep in lakes or not. On a warm, sunny day, however, I do sometimes come across somebody fishing a stream in body waders. Not only does it look odd but the wearer must dehydrate dramatically. As one angler told me as he wrung out his wet socks, he couldn't tell if it was river water or condensation. Today neoprene is the popular wader material, but I look back on the days when Anderson's Scottish rubberised canvas stocking waders were all that you could ever want. John Gierach, writing in *Fly Rod and Reel*, comments that 'Neoprenes—expensive waders that make you wet whether they leak or not— may be an elaborate practical joke.' It may also be a case of back to the drawing board. I don't care, because I don't wear them.

I think a pair of thick woollen socks a good idea when wearing waders. And if you need a wading staff a length of bamboo up to your midriff with a rubber grip is ideal. Drill a hole in it half a metre down and add a nylon cord and dog-clip to attach it to your belt. A metal or rubber end can be dangerous. If anything add a piece of old carpet.

So far as rods go, noted fly-caster Joan Wulff says the choice is 'next in importance to choosing a life's mate.' The factors that direct this choice are price, length, weight and grip, reel seat, bindings and finish. But more important than anything else is action. There *is* a rod that is right for you, its action feeling like an extension of your arm, adding something wonderful to your casting

'On a warm, sunny day'

ability. But *you* are the only one who can select it. Other anglers and advertisements may bring a rod to your attention, but never buy it until you have tried it. Until then you have no basis for comparison; you'll only know which rod suits you when you cast with it, whether you can describe its action or not.

As your experience grows your rod requirements will change and from time to time you will find yourself trying out another rod. I have owned many of them since boyhood, mostly made by Hardy's of England. Today I have three American rods, a Fenwick for wet-fly use and two Sages for the dry-fly. The former is somewhat unique in that it assembles either as a two-piece 9-foot stream rod or a three-piece 11-foot boat rod. One Sage is a 9 foot 6 weight, used chiefly by my wife, the other a 9 foot 7 weight which I find ideal because its power gives me an instant lift-off when I am fishing in tight snaggy corners—a frequent situation which I must say I enjoy. So, as I say, the choice of a rod is a personal affair.

Similarly there are many flylines available but my comments will be brief. The old 'Kingfisher' and 'King Eider' oiled silk lines were excellent and I would be quite happy if they were still in vogue. Instead there is a bewildering choice. Manufacturers constantly try to outdo each other. Eight line-makers market a total of eighty-five models but I will confine my remarks to just four of them.

Airflo does not have my blessing. As Ted Leeson says, 'It's hard to read this company's literature with a totally straight face ... it smacks a bit of scientology, with a host of New Age terms and language guaranteed to confuse.' Rather than amuse me it annoys me. The McKenzie/Borger line is interesting— its bumpy surface skips off the rod-rings minimising contact, and so reducing friction. But as yet it has not been widely used. Cortland have every right to say their 444 is a top line and that it 'stands out from the rest'. But I choose the Aricel Ultra 2 floater for my dry-fly outfit. It casts well and shoots effortlessly, its extra smoothness resulting from making the front and rear tapers longer than normal. In a nutshell it's stiffer, slicker and has a harder finish than any other line. I have little to say about any type of sinking line because I don't use them, but I imagine there's little difference between Cortland, Scientific Anglers and Orvis.

It's hard to discuss lines without thoughts about leaders. But please stay calm. I am not now about to deliver a long and complicated discourse on this much-debated subject. No, what I have to say is short and simple, but based on hundreds of thousands of casts in all weathers over many, many years. I use two leaders, one for the dry-fly, the other for the wet, the former a little longer and finer at the end. I am not concerned with breaking strain; thickness or caliper is of greater importance. In any case makes vary and makers constantly strive to increase breaking strain. On colour I am easily pleased so long as it's not bright, but I reject any brand that curls near the fly after tying it on. At present I prefer 'Umpqua' and 'Steelpower' and my make-ups are as follows:

Dry fly			*Wet fly*		
0.5 mm	765 mm or	30 in	0.5 mm	765 mm *or*	30 in
0.4 mm	685 mm	27 in	0.4 mm	685 mm	27 in
0.3 mm	610 mm	24 in	0.3 mm	610 mm	24 in
0.25 mm	540 mm	21 in	0.25 mm	540 mm	21 in
0.2 mm	540 mm	21 in	0.2 mm	460 mm	18 in
0.16 mm	460 mm	18 in			
		11 ft 9 in			10 ft

Of vital importance is that the leader must be longer than the rod, so that when the fly is hooked in the ring the leader extends through the top runner and is bent through 180 degrees. If the line itself is allowed to do this it will crack and if the temperature is low this will be instant and severe. Any make of line will crack if treated in this way—any make. I've read and heard about all sorts of recipes for leaders made up of all manner or lengths and thicknesses, but it's all like water off a duck's back to me. Some people like to make simple things difficult.

Today there are umpteen fly reels available with an equally wide price range. I need two reels, one for my dry-fly gear, the other for the wet. But I have very decided requirements: both must have a wide drum, must multiply and have a disc drag system. An on-off click is preferable. A tall order, I know, but my Orvis DXR multiplier is a superb dry-fly reel, while my Martin 72 is all I need for wet-fly fishing. The former is ingeniously designed and made, the latter while not so elegant is very functional. Both are American and there is no doubt this country's know-how in fly reel construction leads the world. Various makes like Abel, Aaron, System Two, Winston and many more are superb products. But they don't suit me, that's all.

Fly boxes are of many sorts and sizes. Take your pick, but I can't be bothered with those flip-up lids. Fly floatant is essential—I use 'Permaflote'. Sticky clay will sink a leader like a stone; fill a small pill-container with it. Scissors or nail clippers should be on a string or you'll lose them for sure. A 'priest' and a pair of medical forceps for easy fly removal are both necessary. Since 'Linflot' left the market I find a good line grease hard to obtain. And always stick a

pin or two in your hat to undo wind knots. Some anglers use a net, others don't. But, to my horror, some use a gaff which I cannot accept. I have a light folding telescopic net made by Sharpe's of Aberdeen which I bought in Scotland and it's excellent. A canvas scabbard keeps the net handy and free from tangles. It doesn't matter much what sort of a knife you have so long as it's sharp; there can be little more trying than attempting to clean your catch with a blunt knife. Some people carry a torch, matches and compass. Some a camera and scales. Some always have insect repellant. These are personal things. But only take what you need. I'll tell you what I don't like, however, and that is those sewn-on badges promoting the name of some product or tackle-maker. Man, you do look comical. Has advertising got to the stage where it invades even the peace and loveliness of the stream?

'Peace and loveliness of the stream'

7 Memorabilia

Usually every season there is one particular trout whose undoing is indelibly memorised. Not only this but you can recall the entire event in great detail. I have no trouble in remembering such days forty or more years past. And I'm not talking about huge trout either landed or lost. No, sometimes it's the extreme difficulty overcome that is so unforgettable, or the fight of the fish, or its unusual shape or marking. Perhaps it's badly scarred, or diseased, or something else. But there is only one, or maybe two, of these specials each year. Sometimes there are none at all.

But a year or two ago I did battle with a certain brown trout that will be with me forever. He lived in a sidewater of the South Esk and had a short beat from say two metres immediately below to a little more above a small willow, rarely below, while sometimes he took a little excursion above it, a sort of reconnaissance or tour of inspection. Only, and I mean just that, when he made such a tour was he catchable. But he was as shrewd as they come, with the keenest of eyes that detected the gentlest arrival of the artificial and an uncanny knowledge of drag. If the fly drifted a fraction faster or slower than the current, or moved just a millimetre or two sideways he glared at it with contempt, and me as well. Many times I tried for him. At length it became just a matter of course to see if he was rising, try as best I could, raise my hat to him and move on. I caught fish both below and above him, but from him I got only a frosty stare.

Now, had I been a numbers fisher, he was easy prey at dusk, when the caddis and midges were all over the place and he rose noisily, forgetting his usual college manners as he took insects from the surface with an impeccable sip, leaving a perfect ring regardless of his bulk. But this would have been no way to beat him: it had to be done in daylight. Thus it was on a hot, sultry afternoon when I had the advantage of a milky sky with little wind, that I watched him rising, as usual, beside the willow, quite impossible to catch. My fly was a Red Tag, size 12, and I was in good form as he made his first mistake. Just as I was about to reel up, having had my usual fruitless attempt from below, I noticed his next rise was a bit upstream and the next considerably so. He'd begun one of his tours, giving me my first chance above the willow. With all speed I shifted position, not daring to come closer than peeping distance of the pool. Nor did I dare move a finger. Up to the end of his beat he meandered, rising every minute. Then nothing and I feared the chance had been missed. But then he rose almost in front of the willow close to my side.

Just one backcast I made, dropping the Red Tag a half metre upstream, and waited. The rise was perfect, the fly being clipped from the surface cleanly and silently. I paused, in the true Fred Stewart manner, and then struck firmly. It was like turning on an electric fan—instant and full speed. Forwards he shot and just kept going straight through the weeds and on. You hear about these fish that take you out to your backing. Well, of all the thousands of trout I've played, only two have ever got anywhere near the backing. But never before this, nor since, have I had such a charge. It was like being hooked to a tractor, with a steady unyielding pull. My rod horizontal and applying all the sidestrain I could manage, I was eventually forced to use both hands. Now at the bottom of the next pool, with the line partly submerged in weed, hostilities became hand to hand combat while we slugged it out, me gaining little by little as I won and alternatively lost ground, slowly retrieving until I had him in the lower pool.

I do not care for long drawnout tales of playing a fish. I get bored and glad when it's over. Let me just say that I shall never, so long as I live, forget this grand episode of my fishing days. It was not the stalk, or the extreme difficulty in casting, or the overcoming of fierce drag, or hazardous wading, or any other memorable highlight. It was completely the unbelievable strength and tenacity of the fish that is uppermost in my memory.

Yet there remains a sadness. When the battle was over and he lay vanquished on the short green grass and weed at the side, half in and half out of the water, glistening wet and dark spotted, at a glance exceeding three pounds, I thought about returning him. But what a prize! And had not this doctor friend, whose family enjoyed trout at the table, been badgering me for months for a fish? The temptation was too great. And was it not a choice opportunity to boast? One tap on his noble head was decisive, and that was that.

But oh how often I've regretted it and the remorse has been genuine. I did the wrong thing but learnt from it. That's all I can add. Since then I have become a great supporter of occasional catch and release fishing and every so often can visualise my returning this grand trout to continue living happily in his pool, his right upper jaw clearly showing the marks of some previous tussle, perhaps long ago by the look of it, with either a bait or spinner fisherman whose artfulness he'd beaten after maybe another grand battle, only to fall for my irresistible Red Tag. It would be nice to say, so ends the story, but it does not end. It will always be nostalgic for me.

I said I have become a supporter of occasional catch and release fishing. I fear that if we were to adopt this as a policy we would put ourselves at risk of being one day robbed of our sport by the growing band of animal rights protestors who would be delighted to win the public vote and the power to eventually destroy our sport. Well meant though it may be, as a conservation measure a catch and release policy is self-defeating. Inspired by whatever motive you like, release as many trout as you like, but let us not be committed to doing so.

Like several other words in the English language the meaning of sport has become bent. To the media these days it means not only field sports, but also athletics, football, tennis, golf and all sorts of competitive games. But these are games. You have a game of cricket or a game of soccer. And at the top of the list I guess it's the Olympic Games. But for me 'sport' is clearly defined as hunting, whether with horse and hounds, with dogs, gun or rod. All other pursuits are games. Perhaps I'm splitting straws, but nobody is ever going to tell me that fly-fishing is a game. This is why I classify anglers as sportsmen. It is the policy of catch and release that leads to disaster. It would strip away our credibility as hunters. We would no longer be sportsmen but gamesmen, while the peaceable non-sporting but voting citizens would turn against us.

I cannot explain it. There just does not seem any reason why, whenever I drift into memory of my fishing days, now in the thousands, that I always begin with one day on the Upper Yarra in Victoria, which is now inundated by the Upper Yarra Dam. It was an early summer day, cloudless and warm, as Fred Stewart and I made our way down the steep hillside towards the stream. I had borrowed my father's Vauxhall and picked Fred up at his home near Ringwood. The road to Warburton was sealed, but soon after became rough and dusty when the surface changed to gravel.

The river was clear and cold, running over rounded stones with banks on either side of perhaps half a metre, overhung by ferns or, in some places, long dry grass. There were few trees along this stretch, which turned gently each way, alternately giving a deep and shallow side all the way. As had become our custom we fished turn about, watching each other working the runs and

'Bottom of the next pool'

ripples as we floated a well-hackled Red Tag in every likely spot. These flies I had made myself, using the red neck feathers from a rosella parrot for the tag. The stream held many trout so that each cast was expectant and we were kept busy, returning all but perhaps one in every six caught. It was an unforgettable day ending at a deep slow pool where, after our sandwich lunch, we both took a plump pounder, for this water a goodly specimen. With a bag limit of ten trout each, we trudged up the now wooded hillside towards the car, talking and laughing all the way and filled with a pleasant glow of satisfaction that has rarely been equalled since.

I was on this same stream perhaps a year earlier, alone apart from Mr Chips my cheerful cocker spaniel. And this day too is indelibly etched on my memory because of the incredible emergence of flying termites I encountered. Termites belong to the order Isoptera and are sometimes called white ants. Brown in colour, they leave their home in countless numbers, their wings being about twice as long as their bodies, from which they easily become separated. Swarming usually occurs towards dusk on hot summer evenings, but on this occasion it was a warm humid morning. Apart from hatches of mayflies and to a lesser extent midges, I have never since this day seen so many insects of the same kind at the same time. They were everywhere, all over me and even Mr Chips who viewed them with suspicion. The trout, however, thought the whole thing excellent and rose steadily and noisily.

I was on a favourite length of stream in a secluded corner where an antique trolley line once wended its way beside it, carrying logs to the old sawmill upstream, the faint remains of which, together with the large sawdust heap, was still identifiable. A wooden bridge had once spanned the stream over which the logs were hauled, some of its rotted piers still standing. Below this were several splendid adjoining pools and I remained in this area for the whole morning and a bit more.

My Red Tag was not altogether approved of, nor a Greenwell, but a Wickam's Fancy was accepted with gusto and I had a fine time. Mr Chips enjoyed it too, finding the splashing of the fighting trout and its flapping on the bank most entertaining. Only when a termite landed on his nose was he concerned. Have you ever seen a dog go cross-eyed? He looked somewhat like Pluto and my laughter didn't please him either. The grey fantails, as might be expected, had a royal feast. But I was surprised to see so many yellow robins also making the most of an easy meal. The bigger trout were up too and I think amongst my bag were two or three in the pound and a quarter range.

'Some of its rotted piers still standing'

Is it any wonder that I remember the Upper Yarra with a gentle and sweet melancholy? It has all gone now, another victim of man's insatiable hunger for progress. But my memory will last a little longer, God willing, and these pages a little longer still. Please try to understand me, for angling of this kind doesn't exist any more.

Every so often someone asks me to show them how to fish with a fly. Usually they are all set and ready to go. 'What will I bring?' they ask. To which my answer of 'Just yourself and your lunch' may come as a disappointment, because they have in mind pulling out a trout or two right from the start. By the end of the day, however, it's a different story when they are both fascinated and amazed after watching the whole operation, never really expecting so much to be involved. And always it's the casting and placement of the fly that is of special charm, the striking and playing of the fish not as yet receiving the attention it will surely attract once they get started.

I have read umpteen articles on learning how to cast, and watched videos too, giving a variety of instructions and explanations. They all seem perfectly sound in theory, but when I have tried to teach a learner along these lines I have proved a poor instructor. As a recent student complained, 'It's all just a big confusion!' My own procedure I find much more successful, and have adopted it consistently. I take their rod myself. Try its action, then cast out about two rod lengths and leave the line, leader and old fly lying on the lawn. Then, having demonstrated the right grip, I get them to make one cast only, once back and then forward to land the fly, as best they can, where it came from. There's a lot to be learnt to just achieve this correctly before trying false casting backwards and forwards. In addition it gets them into the habit from the start of not making any more false casts than necessary.

And so, little by little, like learning to ride a bike, they grasp the idea and are soon ready to try themselves out on the stream. Until they have reached this stage I have little or no memory of any of my students but the absolute ecstasy of their first success I do recall. One of the most outstanding was an insurance salesman whom I took to the Lake River. At a splendid pool that I knew of old always carried trout and was easy to fish, I purposely left him and went on ahead. Sure enough it wasn't that long before he came striding round the corner, rod in one hand and net in the other in which a bright-spotted pounder lay vanquished, his beaming smile enough to give me half as much pleasure as his own.

But nothing can take the place of Lord and Lady Rowallan's exhibition. Colin Gibson and I had been guides, as it were, to the then Governor of Tasmania

'Splendid pool that I knew of old'

and his wife for a few days in the highland lakes area. By the last day Lady Rowallan had still been unsuccessful, although had fortune been kind to her she would have landed a fish in a bay at Bronte Lagoon, then known as Woodwards, which now bears their name since our visit to it. Anyway, our final target was Tungatinah Lagoon, and as dusk approached Lady Rowallan, who had waded out some distance, gave a loud screech as the trout that had seized her Watson's Fancy leapt and splashed furiously. 'Hold fast, my dear,' yelled Lord Rowallan, 'I'll bring a net!' And, so saying, he scrambled and sloshed his way out to his still-shouting wife, her rod bent alarmingly as she held on desperately.

Both Colin and I watched anxiously, hoping against hope that all would go well, until finally after an unbelievable muddle mixed with remarkable fortune the fish was netted. This done Lord Rowallan immediately set off for the shore, the still hooked trout thrashing in the net and the line peeling off the reel trailing behind. At length the whole tangled heap of rod, net, line and fish lay on the grass, while the cheerful pair hugged and gazed fondly down at the prize, Lady Rowallan's first trout in Tasmania and also her last. The sigh of relief from Colin and me must surely have had no equal, while there would be much merriment at Government House when the account was given and the event relived.

Basically trout fishermen are of two kinds. It's not a case of whether they fish with dry or wet flies, or fish either rivers or lakes, rich or poor, good mannered or bad. No. Just those who fall in and those who don't. I know one angler who falls in regularly. Mind you, he's a bit venturesome and this no doubt tends to make his ducking more certain. But I want now to be very serious about such misadventure, because first it happened to me and second it may well have ended in tragedy.

It all took place many years ago one morning on the Yarra below Launching Place. It was springtime with a fair amount of water in the stream, not a banker but not far from it. A large old gum had fallen across the river and I decided to use it to reach the other side. Overnight rain had made its smooth surface slippery and about midstream my rubber-soled waders lost their grip. Had I fallen on the downstream side things would just have been wet, but in I went on the upstream side and was swiftly swept under the surface and under the log. Complications set in at once because I struck snags. I abandoned all my tackle and fought for dear life to free myself and get downstream. It was some struggle and a nasty memory. Today I know my Shepherd and as a sheep I have profound thanks for my survival.

I think I managed to break several branches—one's strength is incredible at such times—and so was able to disentangle myself to be carried down under the remaining obstacles, turning over as I went, my hands feeling the stream bottom and my head hitting I don't know what. Then suddenly it was freedom and just swirling water. Instinctively I made for the shallows, by chance heading for the side from which I began crossing. Soon my feet felt bottom and I struggled upright, then slowly heaved myself through and over the muddy edge, there to sit wet and puffed, my rod and most of my gear gone.

So our fishing memories are not always pleasant nor quiet, regardless of the good wishes of dear old Izaak Walton.

Have you ever come across one of those tough old men of the bush, bewhiskered and clad in a faded singlet, ancient trousers, thick leather belt and hob-nailed boots? I have. Several times. They're a part of Australia that is fast dying out. I wish I had the time and opportunity to talk to and record as many as I could. What a golden store of stories I'd have. I have not found one of these oldtimers for years, except an odd one in northeastern Tasmania where there still remain a few. But of them all I remember only two who had never heard of fly-fishing, regarding it with a kind of humorous scepticism, until they saw it practised successfully with their own eyes. Let me tell you about them.

The first came striding along the rough track beside the headwaters of the Big River in Victoria in which Fred Stewart and I were wading and fishing our dry flies, taking the pools in turn, first one and then the other, drifting our Red Tags down the ripples. Sinking his axe into a stump he viewed us with interest, much as you would monkeys at the zoo. Then he called out 'D'yer ever catch anythin'?' To which Fred quickly replied, in his broad Scottish accent, 'My wurrd we do.' The oldtimer seemed even more intrigued by Fred's accent and came down the bank to squat on a big rock at the water's edge. We waded over and so began our *tête-à-tête*.

We talked about anything and everything associated with trouting, his amazement with our tackle growing the more we talked and explained the principles of fly-fishing. But when Fred opened a box of flies and handed it to him for inspection it was a sight I can never forget. As he picked over the flies with hard-worn fingers, carefully lifting some out, there was a look of utter wonderment on his tanned face. I recall only two or three of his remarks accurately and these alone I will quote. 'What little 'ooks,' he said, ''ow d' they 'old?'

Suddenly, he changed the subject. 'I do a bit o' fishin' meself, with bardy grubs.' It was our turn to listen and be instructed. The grubs he used turned out to be wattle grubs, as, with much arm-waving and facial expression he explained his special method in their use. He told us how to read the water as he moved downstream choosing the deep loggy corners. Sometimes he did a little daytime reconnaissance, marking the spots with branches stuck in the bank and then returning in the evening, going from place to place. He used a short old steel rod and 'good thick gut on a fair sized 'ook.' The grub was threaded on tail first, the barb fixed in the tough head and the unweighted bait cast out and allowed to sink down into the dark depths as he searched out each hole. Sooner or later, he assured us, there would be a tightening on the line as a trout grasped the grub. His eyes now narrowed and you could see he was there in his mind, his hands extended, holding an imaginary rod and line. Now he would pay out a little slack and 'let him 'ave a good go at it.' Then, and I can remember it clearly, he held one hand against his stomach and with a look of triumph, ''it 'im an' he's yours.'

And secondly there was the old fellow who lived by himself in a hut near Derby in Tasmania whom Colin Gibson and I came across and who I have a faint idea I mentioned in a previous writing, but not in this connection so it doesn't matter. As a youth he'd been kicked in the face by a horse and was somewhat disfigured and spoke with an impediment but he knew the bushland closely and all its creatures. Indeed, he had a regular family of tame parrots, jays, rabbits and wallabies near his old hut which he fed by hand as we hid behind some nearby tea-trees.

We saw him twice. Once on our way to the stream and afterwards on our way back, when we left our catch with him. His amazement was the same—a complete revelation. But he did not see us in action on the water. Instead he watched in awe as we had a few casts behind his hut, which seemed only to astound him further, because he could not understand how the line could be propelled without a weight on its end. He told us he had attempted to feed rising trout in the river with stale bread, like the other wild things, but without success. It's been a year or two now since I passed that way again. The old hut has gone and all its surrounding paraphernalia—he must have died and, I fondly trust, is now in heaven, where God willing such lovely old men of the backwoods belong, honest, peaceful and at one with the natural world.

Perhaps now for a little poem I learned in the New England parts of America, which goes well with either of these characters. I spent some months there long ago fishing the wooded streams. I even caught bright little brook trout that rose eagerly to the floater and were so lovely a sight when fresh from the water, glistening so prettily.

'Big rock at the water's edge'

Yer won't catch nothin' with them there things,
With yarn fer bodies an' feathers fer wings,
Yer must think trouts is terrible fools
T' be catched with such outlandish tools.

'Well I'll be durn, yer can shoot me dead,
If here aint a windlass filled with thread,
An' the lightst sort o' thread at that
Why, man that wouldn't hold a gnat!

'You'll find a good 'ole over there,
Under the willers, deep an' clear,
But yer better take worms an' a hickory pole,
Or yer won't catch nothin', 'pon me soul.'

Twelve fat beauties speckled bright
The fish bag bore 'ere fall of night
And, as he counted them over on a bank of fern,
All he said was 'Well, I'll be durn.'

You've no idea the things that happen to me.

I'm not talking about the wind that starts just as I arrive. I'm used to that and half expect it anyway. No, but take for example the riser I have fished to with all the skill I can muster without success, maybe resting him for a bit before trying again, and once more drawing a blank; I reel up and hook the fly in the ring. Then, after a final look, just as I turn and take the first step to leave, he rises again in exactly the same place. Do you know that I have gone back and repeated the whole performance a second time! Or else, and this is worse, as you cover the spot as carefully as you can, he is no longer there but suddenly appears cruising straight at you with a nasty smirk on his face. He knows that you know that he knows you're there, and that you can do nothing about it. Or even worse still, by some manner of magic you spot him before he spots you and by still more magic you drop your fly nicely before him. Up to it he comes, while your heart misses two beats, and with the wisdom of Solomon peers at it microscopically before, with a disdainful toss of the head, turns away with a comment like 'If you want me out mate, you'll have to do better than this.' Doubtless you present the fly again, with no response whatever as he slowly disappears. Insolent oaf!

Dry-fly fishing this year has been abnormally plagued by wind and to get any fishing at all it's been a case of when the wind has stopped drop everything and go. So there you are, having thrown prettily across to where a trout has risen against the weeded far edge, perhaps even twice. A heave and leave affair

'Rises again in exactly the same place'

as the Americans say. And there your fly sits attractively. Hopefully you watch it. And still watch it. After a while you sneak a quick look up the straight to your left in search of more action. Nothing, So, it's back to your fly. Then it's a sneak look to your right. Nothing. But, alas, when you return to your fly it's gone, the widening rings marking your blunder. Does this ever happen to you?

The same kind of trouble can happen when you decide to change flies or tie on a new point. A trout that has not risen all day or maybe not all week will now rise a rod and a half's length away. And for me he will rise twice more. It's all very testing. But there's no excuse for that other lamentable business. On a day when no trout rises anywhere, finally a good fish does sidle up to your searching fly and eats it. With confidence you strike, because he puts his whole neb over it and you never miss those. He's on! But now he's off. You pull in to find your hook broken at the bend. Will I ever learn to check my fly? And so, now, with the wind rising you decide you've been blown off and head homewards. But you're not there long and it goes flat calm! Truly, we are wonderful people to keep going.

And another thing: pleased with yourself, having flat sidecast twice with the accuracy of a sharpshooter under the overhanging willow across the far side, where in the slow flow a decent fish has risen noisily a couple of times, you have to retrieve and recast because he's moved up several metres. Now, on the bank over which your line lies—because you have stood back out of sight— amongst the short dry grass there is but one little thistle, a bare five centimetres tall, with a poor shrivelled flower and two or three crinkled leaves. But, as if influenced by a spell, around this your leader goes and there you are, *hors de combat*. A hundred times that day you have lifted off a similar spot cleanly, even with several obstructions, but not this time. The foe now displays his nastiest streak. He knows you're helpless and he's safe, so round he comes, on purpose near the surface so you can see him, right past you, while you go down to the little dessicated weed muttering and cursing. Small it may be, but it still manages to drive a spike into your thumb and forefinger.

But to counter all this misery, about every ten years a miracle takes place. You've done a good throw on a big still pool where a while ago an energetic fish leapt out to seize a wayward damselfly. And, as might be expected you eventually start gazing about. So, not looking at your fly, you make your liftoff backcast and find you've struck to a rise at precisely the right moment!

Then again, the other day the wind, of course, was blowing, yet there were short intervals of less velocity when a rise or two got me excited. Then came a particularly vicious blast over my right shoulder, so without hesitation I gave

'Big still pool'

up and, pointing the rod directly into the teeth of the odious squall so that I might catch and secure the fly, instead I simply lost it. One moment it was fluttering around with me after it and the next it had disappeared. Where was it? Miraculously, it had hooked nicely in the ring, all by itself!

8 Philosophy

It is usual these days, I suppose, when on the road in many parts of Australia, to meet one of those huge, thoroughly objectionable trucks with its ugly load of logs. Two things instantly come to mind: are they sawlogs or pulplogs and where did they come from? The other morning, en route to the river, I met one of these monsters coming in the opposite direction. Its load consisted of just two logs, the pitiful remains of two giant and stately gums that for the greater part of a century had looked out across the timbered valley towards the rugged, rocky hilltop beyond. The sparkling stream below tumbled over stones and flood debris, edged by musk and myrtle, fern and moss. Perhaps the two noble trees had grown close enough together to converse, doubtless discussing the forest and its condition, agreeing that the summer had been abnormally dry and how urgently a decent rain was needed. And who am I to say that these trees are unable somehow to communicate. Are they not alive like you?

They had often seen the pair of eagles riding the thermals over the range and also watched closely the smoke from a lightning-strike fire that passed too close not to cause alarm. For decades they had stood there towards the edge of the sky, with only the sounds of the wind and birds and possums. Occasionally an old dead tree might crash to the ground or thunder roll down the gully, while insects buzzed to and fro. They were an integral part of God's world and totally at peace with it. As Dante Alighieri said, 'Nature is the art of God.'

They had, of late, become aware of man's existence—vaguely at any rate—because of the aircraft that sometimes passed far above, leaving tell-tale vapour trails to drift slowly away. But not until several years ago had they had any close acquaintance, when a few kilometres away a road had been constructed by forestry workers, the grinding and clanking of their heavy machinery hurting the bush.

Thereafter their world changed, for every so often a noisy vehicle whined along this road, the dust hanging in the previously clean air to settle on the rocks and stumps strewn along its sides. Once there had been rifle shots and the voices of men. But the most hideous sound of all had been the staccato of chainsaws and the screaming of the trees and undergrowth as the saws sliced and hacked their way forward, with no care for the death they wrought or the tangled mess they left behind. But logging is always associated with utter disorder and destruction.

So they passed by, these two vast trunks, I think on their way to a sawmill. No ordinary sawmill mark you; it would have to be a big outfit to handle them, as I would estimate their greatest girth at six metres while heaven alone knows their weight. Solid they were, with true heartwood to their centres, their debarked sides showing strong, clean sapwood. And as I did then, I now feel a sadness as I think of the agony of the chainsaw tearing its way through their flesh until, at length, each lofty head shuddered, slowly gathering velocity, to fall crazily earthwards, smashing all before it. Then, beheaded, debarked and rudely dragged to the loading ramp, there to lie with other hapless logs until hoisted gracelessly to the trailer, they go to be reduced to beams and planks. What are we that we make such chaos of everything we touch on earth?

The upland slopes, where these and other trees have been removed, are now completely open to the sun. No longer is there a shaded, damp carpet over the forest floor; instead even the smallest native plants cry out for moisture. And, snaking their way in all directions, are bare earth snig or caterpillar tracks, dry and rough in summer but smelly mud ruts in winter. Saplings and some crooked trees are left amongst the maze of twisted dead branches and bark. No more the virgin bush but a kind of half and half with scattered stumps and bruised wildlife uncertain of the long distances between habitats. This is the scene when an area is logged.

On the return home that same day, in more or less the same place, I met another huge truck with its load of logs. But this time I had no doubt about its destination; the thirty or forty mixed trees that made up its tall cargo were bound for the chipper and then to Japan. Possibly the area they had come from had been clearfelled—in other words totally destroyed—leaving a mangled mass of earth, branches and bark which might then be burnt before being replanted with row upon straight row of quick-growing eucalypts; these in turn to be cut down, the moment they are ready, to feed the chipper. You and I may love old gnarled gums with drooping twisted limbs and jumbled low scrub, with hollows in them providing homes and nests for wildlife. This, for many of us, was the Australia we fought for, and some died for, in time of war. But since then we have progressed.

'Rugged rocky hilltop beyond'

But worst of all, when heavy rain comes these clearfelled slopes suffer sorely. Little trickles unite to form streamlets, that combine to cut deeper and deeper into the soil, washing it downhill to the stream below, turning its clear water into a muddy torrent. No more the straining and slowing effect of the forest floor. No more the wide leafy canopy takes the brunt of wind and rain. More of the hillside is carried to the river and on to the flooded flats, while the trout do their best to cope with the murky scouring spate. No longer does the little stream chatter and murmur joyfully over the pebbles and gurgle over the rocks in miniature waterfalls. Even in winter, after steady rain, while it surely rose in height and its flow increased, its water still remained clear. But now, fed by the uncontrolled input from perhaps several clearfells, it tears down the valley in wild confusion.

That day I also looked in dismay at the many irrigation sprays along the river. In theory their abstraction is limited, but does anyone really know how many billions of litres are hurled over the crops in a single day? Or what this does to the natural ecology of the streams and their inhabitants? And what about the countless introduced willows that line the banks? I have written at some length before in *Ripples, Runs and Rises* concerning this threat. And in the intervening years their alarming spread has gone on regardless. In these two ways our streams are severely depleted while, at the same time, our woodlands are ravaged by logging. Theodore Gordon, that grand old backwoodsman and father of dry-fly fishing in America and creator of the immortal Quill Gordon fly, was greatly distressed by timber destruction and artificial reafforestation in his time. And so am I today.

Stop now and ponder awhile. Dream a little and refresh your mind. See, there's an angler sitting on that grassy bank, old Izaak himself, his tackle beside him, as he gazes across the pool. And what does he say?

> When I would beget content, and increase confidence in the power and wisdom of providence of Almighty God, I will walk in the meadows of some gliding stream, and there contemplate the lilies that take no care, and those very many other little creatures that are not only created but fed—a man knows not how—by the goodness of the God of nature, and therefore trust in Him.
>
> *The Compleat Angler*

I have been trout fishing now for a long time, ranging widely throughout Australia and in a number of overseas countries. I have met and fished with many people of all ages and both sexes, from office boys to supreme court judges, from wharf labourers to company directors, the unemployed to state governor. Over fifty years have come and gone since my first outing on the Yarra River

'Over the rocks in miniature waterfalls'

at Launching Place in Victoria—a one-shop town then with a railway station and small hotel.

Today, looking back over all the thousands of trout taken after even more thousands of casts, covering thousands of kilometres and thousands of days, what have I to say about fly-fishing? I will not attempt to resolve or define why I go fly-fishing or list its attributes and delightful virtues. I have done this in previous writings. No, but let me tell you that there is what I see as a definite spirit to fly-fishing, the essential stuff or heart and soul of it, that can only become an indwelling part of the fisher through experience. Add to this the personality of the angler and his skills. Without all three being on the credit side the balance sheet is in the red. There is no other way. To have a minus in any one of the three requirements will not do. The company has not been many it is true, but to have known them and fish with them has been a sheer joy. Most of those I have known have, alas, made their last cast and unfortunately amongst the new crop of fly-fishers growing up there do not appear to be many who might join this great band. The old brigade has almost died out and fly-fishing is the loser.

Several times I have had the good fortune and memorable experience of fishing for wild brown trout on private waters in Britain. There is nothing snobbish or aristocratic about it; it's simply that the owner of the property owns the land beneath the river as well as the fields beside it. He may not own the air above the land or the water that flows over it, but he owns the fishing rights and it is trespassing to go on that land without permission. One cannot even go walking there, far less fishing, shooting or mushrooming.

Here in Tasmania the law covering stream fishing is somewhat similar, but not entirely clear. The popularly held belief that an angler may walk along the bank or wade upstream from a bridge provided he does not get out on the bank is simply not true. A landowner in Tasmania may lawfully deny access to the stream, but cannot charge a fee if he does grant it. The water and fish belong to the state, but without permission from the landowner an angling licence does not permit you to angle for them!

Our British forefathers brought many pests to Australia: rabbits, foxes, starlings, perch, thistles, blackberries, gorse and more. Unfortunately they did not bring with them their angling laws, and there is a certain amount of confusion. But when I think, say, of the Kennet above Ramsbury Mill, or below Ramsbury Manor Arches, or parts of the Wyle, there just isn't any comparison. It's like trying to compare a Holden with a Rolls Royce. Mind you, by the same token, there is nothing to compare with the screech of a rosella parrot,

'Running water fishing'

the crackle of dry gum bark underfoot or the unique scent of the Australian bush after rain. Nothing.

Fishing private water overseas is often by invitation, as has been my good fortune, there being no charge, otherwise the fee varies according to the length of stream available, the quality of the fishing, the time of year and the time spent fishing. Normally fly-fishing only is allowed, sometimes limited to the use of the dry fly. This will come to Australia bit by bit. At first there will be a wide range of public water, but as time goes by, where the landowner can control it and where the fishing is of a high enough standard, private water will be established, especially stillwaters and artificially excavated ponds. In the main these will be stocked with hatchery-reared rainbow trout and, according to the size of the fishery, the use of artificial lures will be permitted in larger reservoirs.

Angling competitions will take place between teams, rather like football matches, with teams sponsored by tackle makers, breweries and wineries. But just as surely, private fishing will be instituted, where you or I can go to enjoy the style of fly-fishing we prefer. Our daily bag will be limited, sometimes to a brace or two, or the fishing may be catch and release. In either case it will be a user-pays arrangement. You may not like the sound of it, but both groups of anglers will be catered for—the numbers people and those who desire the real thing. In addition, because money and competition are involved, fishery improvement will be undertaken to attract more customers.

There are one or two other possibilities: where, for example, water is discharged from a reservoir for downstream domestic use, hydro-electric generation or irrigation, if angling restrictions are imposed and policed, and the angler pays a small fee for his sport, there would seem to be hope for some kind of running water fishing. This fishing might, of course, be affected by the artificial raising and lowering of water level as flow rates allow. But beggars can't be choosers, and unless we own or have access to private stream fishing, lovers of this kind of angling must soon learn to beg.

So, another year is over. Another season dawns. I trust I shall be granted another interlude in which to enjoy the magic of the stream and the riches of good companionship. But it's not the same hope that once set me dreaming. With the passing of each year I grow more fearful that the lifestyle which I have enjoyed and laboured to protect may be snatched away and I shall be powerless to prevent it. The wilderness is shrinking and I am well aware that what I once knew as solitude, which I need in large and regular doses and without which I become fretful, is an illusion. Just over the hill I know there is a road, a telephone and an hotel with good food, whisky and private TV. In addition

'Just over the hill'

the publican is genial, the waitress pretty and at the end of the day the bed is warm and comfortable.

I find one of the most pleasant facets of our art is being able to talk about it afterwards, especially on cold, wet, winter nights before the fire. Which is why I seek out the comradeship of like-minded anglers. The thought that this way of life might be ending is too soul destroying to contemplate.

But I was greatly encouraged recently, after talking about the future of fly-fishing with a close angling friend. He is younger and more in touch with current attitudes and is quite confident that anglers themselves will take care that futuristic devices and practices will not encroach upon or alter the jewel we have cultivated and grown to love. I do hope so, because there are large numbers of people out there who have never seen a trout and would not be overly concerned if they all became impregnated with mercury, or dioxin, or DDT. We fishermen need to be seen as environmentally friendly people, but fiercely unshakable in our beliefs, as well as harmless, unfathomable cranks.

Index